Alexander S. Belenky

How America
Chooses Its Presidents

Bloomington, IN  Milton Keynes, UK
authorHOUSE®

AuthorHouse™
1663 Liberty Drive, Suite 200
Bloomington, IN 47403
www.authorhouse.com
Phone: 1-800-839-8640

AuthorHouse™ UK Ltd.
500 Avebury Boulevard
Central Milton Keynes, MK9 2BE
www.authorhouse.co.uk
Phone: 08001974150

First published by AuthorHouse 4/9/2007

ISBN: 978-1-4208-4854-0 (sc)
ISBN: 978-1-4259-9293-4 (hc)

Library of Congress Control Number: 2006910754

Printed in the United States of America
Bloomington, Indiana

This book is printed on acid-free paper.

To the memory of my parents,

Sofia M. Belenkaya and Solomon Y. Belenki

About the Electoral College

The way America elects its presidents has been controversial since the early years of the Republic.

— Prof. Alexander Keyssar, John F. Kennedy School of Government, Harvard University

The mode of appointment of the Chief Magistrate of the United States is almost the only part of the system ... which has escaped without severe censure ... I venture somewhat further, and hesitate not to affirm, that if the manner of it be not perfect, it is at least excellent.

— Alexander Hamilton, The Federalist, N.68, March 14, 1788

It's a ridiculous setup, which thwarts the will of the majority, distorts presidential campaigning and has the potential to produce a true constitutional crisis.

— "Abolish the Electoral College," The New York Times, Editorials/ Opinion, August 29, 2004

With another close presidential contest in store, that hardy if indecipherable oddity of American Politics, The Electoral College, is back in the news.

… The Constitution requires someone to win a majority of electoral votes; otherwise, the House chooses a president from the top three finishers.

How do you think the public would react to the discovery that in such a contingent election, each state delegation has one vote, regardless of its size-the Democratic majority from California being matched by the single Republican member from Delaware? …

… I suspect this whole Electoral College issue is due for serious debate … .

— David Broder, Columnist, The Washington Post, "Electoral College Alternatives Deserve Careful Scrutiny," The Seattle Times, October 21, 2004

I would predict that 200 years from now, we will still have the Electoral College.

— President Jimmy Carter, Co-Chair, National Commission on Federal Election Reform, Transcripts of the First Public Hearing, March 26, 2001, Carter Center, Atlanta, GA

If we never talk about the Electoral College, we will remain stuck with it for another two centuries.

— Prof. Jack Rakove, Department of Political Science, Stanford University

Contents

Preface

"How America Chooses Its Presidents" is the author's second book dealing with the logical analysis of the system of electing a US President. The author's first book on this subject, "Extreme Outcomes of US Presidential Elections" [1], combines features of both a monograph and a textbook on extreme situations that may emerge in US Presidential elections. As a result, the first book contains numerous details on the election system that may interest scholars in the field more than US voters who would like to understand how the system works and why it works as it does. Therefore, the author decided to write a new book, a much smaller volume, to spotlight important aspects of the election system for a general readership. This new book covers all the election rules discussed in the first book and uses "Extreme Outcomes of US Presidential Elections" as a reference source for a more extensive treatment of particular aspects of the system.

Two questions on US Presidential elections have always concerned many US voters:

a) Should the Electoral College remain, or should it be abolished and replaced with a direct popular election system?

b) Should an elected US President have a mandate directly from the American people?

These important questions require, however, certain clarifications. In the first question, it is unclear if the Electoral College is understood as an assembly of particular people (electors) or as a mechanism for electing a US President. The answer may vary depending on how this is construed.

Many US voters believe that theoretical research in the field of US Presidential elections should constitute grounds for the answer to the second question. However, this answer solely depends on whom US voters would like to elect to the office of US President at a particular time in American history.

Answering these two questions requires explanations of the fundamentals of the election system. Based on these explanations, a US voter can juxtapose what he or she expects from the system and what this system currently provides. Therefore, discussing these fundamentals, along with extreme election outcomes, extreme campaign strategies, extreme election strategies, and even stalemates in the elections, is one of the main purposes of this book.

It is obvious that any elections, including US Presidential elections, can be considered fair only if the election rules are clear to the voters in advance. Also, these rules should cover traditionally expected situations in the elections, along with unexpected but logically possible ones. Such unexpected situations in US Presidential elections are called extreme situations (in this book and in the first book [1]). They are caused by logical flaws that are present in the provisions of the US Constitution and Federal Statutes relating to US Presidential elections, as well as by certain election issues not addressed in these documents.

As long as nobody knows what election rules will be applied if certain situations occur, rules of US Presidential elections remain fuzzy. These fuzzy rules may cause weird election outcomes that could be perceived as unfair and could even be contested in the courts.

From the author's viewpoint, extreme situations in US Presidential elections *should be analyzed and dealt with preemptively.* The analysis of such situations, presented in "Extreme Outcomes of US Presidential Elections" [1] and in this book, is *aimed at warning the American electorate of the danger of possible undesirable developments in the elections.* This analysis emphasizes that the existing election system has the potential to cause undesirable situations in the elections no matter how remote or unlikely they may currently seem. The analysis is based entirely on common sense, and understanding its results does not require any special knowledge.

It seems important to emphasize that the US Constitution and Federal Statutes were written *for the American people* rather than only for constitutional lawyers. Therefore, any discrepancies detected in these documents should be pointed out to the American electorate in a form understandable to every US voter. This book, along with the first book [1], attempts to do this.

Logical flaws in the provisions of the US Constitution relating to US Presidential elections require explanations that can be made only by the US Supreme Court. However, this does not mean that the Court can provide explanations of all these flaws in principle. As a result, certain corrections to the election rules may be possible only in the framework of a new amendment to the US Constitution.

At the same time, it is interesting to notice that even the automatic plan of counting electoral votes, suggested by political leaders and scholars in the field, has failed to be introduced [2]. Some reformers have considered this plan to be too small an issue to go to the trouble of writing a new amendment to the US Constitution. Although introducing this plan could eliminate many extreme election outcomes that are discussed in this book, the plan could be introduced only if the US Supreme Court established that the (assumed) freedom of electors to vote their own choice means their obligation to follow the will of the states and the District of Columbia (DC), which they represent in the Electoral College. It seems (at least to the author) that such a "small issue" combined with other issues relating to the election rules to be discussed in this book may, eventually, "tip the scale" in favor of developing a new amendment to the US Constitution. This new amendment could clarify the existing rules of US Presidential elections and correct already recognized discrepancies and logical flaws in these rules.

In addition, new issues associated with the continuity of the US Government, which emerged as a result of the September 11, 2001 tragedy, have recently been discussed in the light of the existing Presidential Succession Act. The act does not address these issues in certain extreme but logically possible situations [3]. Moreover, the applicability of this act to situations associated with the unpredictability of the voting behavior of electors may, eventually, be questioned. Indeed, it is not clear how a Federal Statute can determine rules of US Presidential elections in situations for which the US Constitution does not authorize the US Congress to provide anything by law (see Chapter 3). From the author's viewpoint, all the above-mentioned issues at least deserve to be publicly debated.

Also, this book discusses the conceptions of "President of the people," "President of the states," and "President of an electoral majority in the Electoral College," introduced in "Extreme Outcomes of US Presidential Elections" [1] and outlined in this book. The comprehension of these three conceptions of the US Presidency can help the reader better understand basic principles underlying the election system.

The closer the next election is, the more intensive are the debates on the existing election system. However, as long as nobody explains to

US voters in a simple manner how the system works, these debates will be left to political propagandists, often pursuing their own agendas, scholars in the field, and media reporters. This is especially the case once unexpected developments take place in the election as a result of applying fuzzy election rules.

In addition, some false though plausible statements about the Electoral College, the key element of the existing election system, become possible. These statements are embedded in the people's minds and not refuted even by those whom they hurt the most. The statement that without the Electoral College, a (particular) Democratic candidate could "buy" US Presidential elections in the populous states was aired many times in the year 2000. Although this statement may seem plausible, it was proven to be incorrect [1]. However, the statement has never been refuted either by leaders of the Democratic party or by any Democratic analysts. Thus, due to an insufficient understanding of the Electoral College both by those who aired the statement and by the analysts, the (assumed) intent to favor the Electoral College resulted in a misleading action that diverted the attention of US voters from the true value of this key election mechanism [1].

The analysis of unexpected situations that may emerge in US Presidential elections, undertaken in the first book [1], has helped detect two issues that should concern every US voter. The first one is a logical mistake that is present in the text of Article 2 of the US Constitution (see the first book [1] and Chapter 3 of this book). Certainly, this mistake cannot any longer affect outcomes of US Presidential elections as a clause from Amendment 12 of the US Constitution superseded the clause from Article 2 of the US Constitution containing the mistake. Nevertheless, the presence of this mistake in the text of the Supreme Law of the Land without any comment seems to be inappropriate. The author has tried many times to draw public attention to this issue by sending copies of "Extreme Outcomes of US Presidential Elections," along with letters explaining the mistake, to both US authorities and the media. Nevertheless, these efforts have so far failed.

The second issue is associated with the potential failure to elect a US President and a US Vice President by inauguration day by both the Electoral College and the US Congress. This failure may cause a constitutional crisis in the country should the applicability of the Presidential Succession Act in this situation be questioned and not be confirmed by the US Supreme Court. As Chapter 3 argues, Section 3 of the Twentieth Amendment of the US Constitution authorizes the US Congress to provide by law for the situation in which " ... neither a President elect nor a Vice President elect shall have qualified ..." rather than for the one in which both executives shall not have been chosen by inauguration day. Moreover, the language employed in the section suggests that situations in which " ... the President shall not have been chosen before the time fixed for the beginning of his term ..." and " ... the President elect shall have failed to qualify ..." are treated differently [5].

Whether this constitutional crisis would emerge depends, however, on whether the phrase "the Vice-President" from the Twelfth Amendment should be attributed to the Vice President-elect rather than to the acting one (see Chapter 3 for the details).

Interestingly, public attention has never been drawn to this situation by specialists and scholars in the field. The uncertainty associated with the applicability of the Presidential Succession Act in the case under consideration has remained since 1947. Also, an uncertainty associated with the interpretation of the language employed in the Twelfth Amendment has existed since 1804. Both uncertainties are illustrative of problems that the country may face in US Presidential elections in the years to come. These problems should be analyzed and dealt with preemptively as fuzzy election rules may cause unexpected situations having the potential of leading to a constitutional crisis in the country.

Neither reading this book nor reading the first book [1] may directly affect the decision of a US voter in a particular US Presidential election. At the same time, the author hopes that both books will contribute to convincing US voters of the value of voting in US Presidential elections by explaining how the election system works. In any case, this book may help the readers better understand topics to be discussed in the course of every election campaign. It may also encourage them to rely on common sense and their own knowledge of the election system's fundamentals rather than only on opinions of particular experts in this field or political propagandists.

The author would like to make it clear that the logical analysis of the election system presented in the book is based solely on the US Constitution, Federal Statutes, and US Supreme Court decisions. Unlike many scholars in the field, the author does not analyze historical materials on the matter. He believes that articles published by some of the Founding Fathers reflect no more than the viewpoints of their authors. These viewpoints *cannot be considered as those shared by a majority of the participants of the Constitutional Convention* no matter how plausible the opposite may seem. The same seems to be true even regarding the Journal of the Constitutional Convention (especially taking into account the history of its publication [4]), which was not signed by a majority of the participants.

In addition, this book does not present the author's viewpoint on the discussed issues. Rather, it contains the logical analysis of these issues based on the above-mentioned documents. This approach reflects the author's intention to provide the reader with basic facts relating to the election system and to offer the logical analysis of these facts rather than to force certain conclusions upon the reader. The author believes that this approach may contribute to making the reader more critical in comprehending facts in general and those presented in this book in particular.

At the same time, certain beliefs of others on related matters are sometimes mentioned or analyzed.

Certainly, if the reader became more critical in analyzing facts as a result of reading this book, the author would consider this book a success. The author also believes that the logical analysis of a particular system, the system of electing a US President, may encourage the readers to develop their own ability to think logically, which will be rewarded many times throughout their lives. Finally, the author hopes that this book will be a helpful introduction to logical analysis, an effective tool for acquiring knowledge.

The author would like to express his appreciation to those who have encouraged his research in the field of the logical analysis of the election system.

A letter from US Vice President Richard Cheney and Lynne Cheney concerning "Extreme Outcomes of US Presidential Elections" [1] convinced the author that the logical analysis of the election system could interest US voters and persuaded him to write the present book. Encouraging letters from President Jimmy Carter and from President Bill Clinton on "Extreme Outcomes of US Presidential Elections" strengthened the author's intention to address the logical fundamentals of the election system in the present book. A valuable discussion of certain election rules with Senator Bob Dole and an encouraging letter from Governor Arnold Schwarzenegger concerning "Extreme Outcomes of US Presidential Elections" emphasized the importance of addressing these fundamentals.

Favorable responses to "Extreme Outcomes of US Presidential Elections" were received from Dr. Norman Ornstein (American Enterprise Institute) and from Prof. David King (John F. Kennedy School of Government, Harvard University), nationally recognized experts and scholars in the field of US Presidential elections. Their encouragement affected the author's decision to publish this book in the present form. Fruitful discussions of the Electoral College mechanism with Prof. David King, a brilliant political scientist who possesses deep knowledge of the subject and combines analytical approaches to studying election systems with the experimental evaluation of new ideas in the field, helped the author choose the structure of the book. Prof. Ervin Rodin (Washington University, St. Louis), a nationally recognized scholar and teacher in the field of systems analysis and applied mathematics, has always encouraged the author's research and its applications. His attention to the author's work in applications of systems analysis to US Presidential elections has been an important factor in developing new results in this field.

Iourii Belenkii and Ilya Belenkiy were instrumental in helping the author in the preparation of the book. Valuable discussions of the election system with Iourii Belenkii helped the author clarify certain logically possible viewpoints expressed by others on matters relevant to the subject of the book. Ilya Belenkiy rendered valuable technical assistance in developing the manuscript. Particular aspects of US Presidential elections were discussed with Dr. James Green, a writer and a highly qualified editor. His views on the election system as a voter and a specialist in the US Government and political science helped concentrate the author's attention on certain aspects of the system that might interest the American electorate the most.

Constructive discussions of ideas underlying the election system with Dr. Mikhail Zalmanov, who has supported the author's research in the field of US Presidential elections since its very beginning and has helped organize a promotional campaign for "Extreme Outcomes of US Presidential Elections," affected the selection of the material that the author decided to include in this book. Mark Belenkii was invaluable in helping the author comprehend views of young American voters on the election system and in organizing promotional campaigns for the author's books on US Presidential elections.

The author has learned a lot about wording and writing style from Gay Haldeman, a distinguished editor and writing consultant, as a result of consulting services rendered by MIT's Writing Center. Both James Green and Gay Haldeman answered a number of questions on wording and punctuation posed by the author in the course of working on the book. Though the author almost always followed advice of these two editing experts, he would like to make it clear that he is solely responsible for the text of the book.

The creativeness, initiative, and attentiveness of Jennifer Handy, who supervised the design of the book, were instrumental in preparing the book for publication.

The author would like to express his gratitude to Philadelphia Daily News, The Boston Globe, The Carter Center, The New York Times, and The Washington Post for the permissions to use quotations from their publications relating to the Electoral College. Finally, special thanks go to Late Show with David Letterman, which drew the author's attention to the system of electing a US President and motivated his research of this system. The research led to the writing of both "Extreme Outcomes of US Presidential Elections" and the present book.

Newton, Massachusetts,

January 2007

Introduction

Different people often perceive outcomes of certain events differently, and US Presidential elections are illustrative of this. Four times in American history, the elected US President did not receive even a plurality of the nationwide popular vote, and many US voters perceived each such outcome as undesirable. In addition, the intervention of the US Supreme Court in the 2000 Election decided the election outcome. Certainly, many US voters did not expect such a development.

"How America Chooses Its President" considers outcomes of US Presidential elections that are undesirable for and unexpected by a substantial part of society. Studying such outcomes, called extreme election outcomes in this book, will help explain why they may occur. Also, it seems important to find out what might be done to eliminate them.

Rules employed in the existing election system are what may cause extreme election outcomes. If these rules are not clear, and their applicability can be contested, chances of extreme or weird election outcomes increase. Therefore, comprehending the election rules, as well as the other fundamentals of the election system, is the key to eliminating extreme election outcomes.

Changes in the election system or the replacement of this system with a new one may eliminate extreme election outcomes or reduce their chances of occurrence. However, this does not mean that these changes or the replacement can be justified. First, the changes may cause new extreme election outcomes that can be even worse than those eliminated by the changes. Second, changing or replacing the existing system makes sense only if a modified or a new election system will serve society better than the old one. Third, any reasonable modifications of the existing system or new election systems may not eliminate certain extreme election outcomes.

Detecting possible extreme election outcomes and their dependency on the system's structure and the election rules seems helpful. In particular, this may help avoid situations in which the election rules must be changed or modified while the election is in progress. Such an approach to improving the election system would undoubtedly make elections fairer.

US voters expect that eligible US citizens will be elected or selected to the offices of US President and US Vice President as a result of each US Presidential election. However, neither may be possible. This means that the election cannot be completed in accordance with the rules determined by the US Constitution [5] and Federal Statutes [6]. This book considers such situations, called stalemates. Certainly, stalemates in US Presidential elections are undesirable, so fair election rules should make them impossible.

Changes in the existing election system can be made in the form of new amendments to the US Constitution and in the form of new Federal Statutes. Making changes in either form requires certain procedures that are hard to initiate and complete. Therefore, one should not expect that even if the changes were reasonable, they could be made quickly. However, addressing extreme election outcomes and the stalemates could encourage substantive discussion of the existing election system. This discussion may either lead to changes in the system or, vice versa, show that any changes are unreasonable or even harmful. Either result would help US voters better comprehend the existing election system.

A particular interpretation of certain election rules stipulated by the US Constitution may cause extreme outcomes of US Presidential elections, and this book considers such outcomes. Decisions of the US Supreme Court that interpret these election rules can, however, eliminate chances of these extreme outcomes without changing the US Constitution.

Existing election rules should be explained and new election rules should be declared and explained before the election starts. *US voters have the right to know what election rules will be exercised in extreme situations.* However, the existing election rules remain fuzzy [1].

US Presidential candidates are players in "the election game," and they play by fuzzy rules that govern this game. Constitutionally, US Presidential elections can be won either via the Electoral College or via the US Congress. As a result, the runner-up or the candidate who won the least number of electoral votes may have a chance to be elected to the office of US President. This book describes certain extreme election strategies that lead to such election outcomes and that are not prohibited by the existing rules.

This book describes detected possible extreme outcomes, stalemates, extreme campaign strategies, and extreme election strategies in US Presidential elections. In addition, the book outlines and logically analyzes the fundamentals of the system of electing a US President and explains which of its parts may cause these phenomena in US

3

Presidential elections. Finally, the book discusses certain modifications that can be made within the existing system, as well as those of the system itself. These modifications could eliminate detected extreme election outcomes and stalemates and reduce the temptation to employ extreme strategies. At the same time, the author would like to clarify what the readers should not expect from this book and will not find in it.

1. Many scholars in the field of US Presidential elections and the Electoral College usually take a position on the election system (see, for instance, "The Electoral College Primer 2000" [7]). Unlike them, the author, a Ph.D. in systems analysis and applied mathematics, does not take such a position. Rather, he describes how this system works and explains why it works as it does. The author does not render any judgments on how good or how bad the system is. Rendering such judgments locally implies that there are certain parameters that reflect the quality of the system's work and are widely accepted by society. However, the author is not aware of such parameters.

2. The book considers certain possible changes within the existing system and modifications of the system itself. At the same time, there are no author's judgments on whether these changes and modifications should be made. Rendering such judgments logically implies that there are certain criteria for comparing election systems and that these criteria are widely accepted by society. However, the author is not aware of any such criteria.

3. The election system designed by the Constitutional Convention participants and the current one are no longer the same [1]. This book discusses and emphasizes the differences between these two systems. At the same time, any evaluations of the degree of similarity or difference between these systems lie beyond the scope of this book. It seems that, currently, such evaluations can be discussed only at the level of

subjectivity or personal preferences. However, throughout the book, the author tries to avoid any such discussions.

4. The book does not address historical details and circumstances surrounding the evolution of the election system. The reader interested in them is referred, in particular, to "The People's President. The Electoral College in American History and the Direct-Vote Alternative" [8].

5. Numerous modifications of the election system have been proposed for more than two hundred years. This book does not review these proposals. The reader interested in studying them is referred to "The Electoral College and the Constitution: The Case for Preserving Federalism"[2] and to "Choosing a President. The Electoral College and Beyond" [9]. The originals of the proposals can be found in the Congressional Record. Some modifications of the election system close to those proposed in this book and in "Extreme Outcomes of US Presidential Elections" [1] are, however, cited.

6. A President-elect and a Vice President-elect can make unexpected decisions in the course of the election, which may cause unexpected election outcomes. Tragic events in the course of the election can cause weird election outcomes as well. Such election outcomes are not considered in this book. The interested reader can find their analysis in "After the People Vote: a Guide to the Electoral College" [6]. By definition, these election outcomes are extreme. However, in this book, the author concentrates only on the logical analysis of certain elements of the existing election system. He analyzes how the expressed will of US voters, presidential electors, and members of the US Congress can cause extreme outcomes and stalemates in US Presidential elections.

7. No analysis of voting technologies and types of voting machines that are in use in the precincts throughout the country is provided in the book. Though these technologies and machines caused the controversy in the 2000 Election, they do not affect the election

rules. Rather, they affect the process of auditing the votes cast, a process that has been widely discussed in society since the 2000 Election. Introducing the so-called provisional ballots and options to vote via the Internet fall into the same category of problems that do not directly affect the election rules. Therefore, these voting options are not discussed in the book either.

Finally, a few remarks on the presentation of the material are in order.

a) The author uses current values of the parameters of the election system in all the reasoning throughout this book. For instance, the numbers of electoral votes allocated to the states and to the District of Columbia (DC) and the numbers of all electors that can be appointed are those established for the period 2001–2010. A particular US Presidential election is sometimes called *the* US Presidential election to emphasize that the election is considered under these particular values of the parameters.

b) Both in "Extreme Outcomes of US Presidential Elections" [1] and in this book, the author sometimes does not adhere to the terminology that is traditionally used in books on US Presidential elections. For instance, such phrases as "the number of the received electoral votes is a majority of all the appointed electors" (see similar phrases in "After the People Vote: a Guide to the Electoral College" [6]) are not used in the book. Instead, the author uses the phrases " electoral votes received from electors who constitute a majority of all the appointed electors" and "a majority of the electoral votes that are in play in the election." In addition, the author calls the states and the District of Columbia the places, meaning the parts of the country eligible to appoint electors in US Presidential elections. This helps avoid distinguishing the states from the District of Columbia in the Electoral College when all of them are considered only from the viewpoint of the number of electors that they are entitled to.

c) Throughout the book, the author uses extensively such words and phrases as "it seems," "in particular," "may," "apparently." He does this to emphasize that all the statements that have not been proven can be considered only as possible viewpoints of their authors no matter how plausible these statements may seem. In "Extreme Outcomes of US Presidential Elections" [1], a book oriented to a broad spectrum of active US voters, the author viewed the extensive use of these words as a deficiency. However, studying recent publications on US Presidential elections convinced him that it was, in fact, a merit of the book. Moreover, based on his personal experience, the author would like to recommend to the readers this style of setting forth any matters. This style may help them avoid the unexpected criticism and unjustified pressure of various opinionated opponents, especially in discussions conducted at the level of subjectivity and personal preferences.

d) The styles of the presentation of the material in "Extreme Outcomes of US Presidential Elections"[1] and in this book are substantially different. Each sentence from the first book was written with the intention of excluding ambiguities in interpretation. Such an approach requires a certain concentration from the readers as some of the sentences are lengthy. At the same time, only the readers who enjoy or become used to analyzing why a particular word is employed in a sentence, and what purpose it serves are likely to understand the existing election system in depth.

In contrast, the present book is written for a general readership though understanding some of its sections in depth still may require concentration from the readers. However, the simplification of the structure of certain sentences in the book may have led sometimes to ambiguities in their interpretation, which meticulous readers may find. Should this happen, consult "Extreme Outcomes of US Presidential Elections"[1] to resolve them.

Unlike other authors writing on US Presidential elections, throughout the book, the author calls US citizens eligible to vote in these elections US voters rather than simply voters. This helps avoid the confusion that some readers may experience with the notion "voter," which is traditionally construed as a US citizen eligible to vote in all Federal elections, as, currently, not every US voter is necessarily a voter in this customary sense. Indeed, for instance, a US citizen of age 18 or older residing in the District of Columbia is an eligible US voter as he or she is eligible to vote in US Presidential elections in DC. However, this person currently cannot vote in other Federal elections anywhere else in the country in November of a US Presidential election year as this person can register to vote only either in one of the 50 states or in DC. Thus, an eligible US voter registered to vote in DC in a US Presidential election is not a voter in the above-mentioned customary sense in the election year. Technically, however, this person still can vote in midterm Federal elections if he or she meets the requirements to register to vote in a state at the time of the midterm elections. (Currently, interested individuals with places to live both in DC and in at least one state can reregister to vote in a state due to changing the place of residence from DC to this state and then switch the registration back to DC by the time of a US Presidential election.)

Also, for the sake of exactness, throughout the book, the author uses the phrases "US Presidential candidate" and "US Vice Presidential candidate" instead of, for instance, the phrases "Presidential candidate" and "Vice Presidential candidate," respectively, traditionally used in books on US Presidential elections. He does this to distinguish candidates who are on the ballot in a US Presidential election—in particular, candidates nominated by political parties—from party candidates and independent candidates trying to be on the ballot, who may, eventually, campaign until the nomination process is over.

Finally, most of the time, the author uses the phrase "US Presidential election" rather than simply "presidential election" to emphasize the Federal rank of this election though constant reminder may irritate some readers.

Chapter 1

The election system:
from the beginning to the present

This chapter discusses seven developments that have shaped the US Presidential election system over more than two hundred years.

1. *Article 2 of the US Constitution: the initial design of the system.*

Article 2 of the US Constitution introduces the system that was approved by the Constitutional Convention participants in 1787. This system was designed as a three-level election system, and some elements of it are still in force. However, not everything approved in 1787 remains part of the election system today. To emphasize the difference, the author italicizes key verbs in the text of this section of the book. The present tense of an italicized verb means that the election rules described with the use of this verb are in force today, whereas the past tense of an italicized verb indicates the opposite.

At the first level, electors *are* to be appointed, and Section 1 of the article imposes restrictions on candidates to the office of elector [5]. The legislature of each state *chooses* the manner in which the state electors are appointed. In the course of the discussion, participants in the Constitutional Convention suggested various manners of choosing electors by the states [8], [10]. Choosing electors by popular vote in a state *can* be one such manner. The article also *determines* the structure of the Electoral College, a set of all the electors that can be appointed in each US Presidential election, by specifying quotas of state electors.

The number of electors to be appointed in each state *remains* a part of the compromise agreed to by the Constitutional Convention participants. This very compromise led to the creation of the Electoral College. The Founding Fathers agreed that the number of electors of a state in a US Presidential election would equal the total number of the US Senators and Representatives that the state would be entitled to in the US Congress at the time of the election. Section 2 of Article 1 of the US Constitution determines the manner in which the number of state Representatives *was* to be calculated. Section 3 of Article 1 of the US Constitution determines that each state *is* entitled to two US Senators.

At the second level, all the members of the Electoral College appointed in a particular election year *are* to vote on one and the same day. (This day was established by Federal Statute [6] and has remained such ever since.) Each elector *was* to vote in his state for two persons as President, at least one of whom should not be an inhabitant of the elector's state. It is important to emphasize that the US Constitution does not operate with the notion of "US Presidential candidate." Therefore, by casting ballots in favor of particular persons, electors, in fact, *attributed* the status of US Presidential candidate to these persons. The article does not, however, specify which particular persons electors *were* to vote for. The only requirement was to vote by ballot. The voting procedure in each state *was* to result in compiling a list of all the persons voted for as President in which the number of (electoral) votes received by each such person *was* to be indicated.

At the third level, the US Congress *was* to count electoral votes cast in favor of all the persons as President. A list of all these persons with the indication of the number of electoral votes received by each person *was* to be prepared, and this list was supposed to be ordered. Namely, if none of the persons on the list was a recipient of electoral votes from a majority of all the appointed electors, only "... the five highest on the List ..." [5] *were* entitled to be further considered by the House of Representatives. Certainly, such a majority of electoral votes *could not* be received by more than three persons. However, three persons among those voted for as President *could* receive such a majority each [1], and the following example is illustrative of this statement.

Example 1. Let us consider the 1800 US Presidential election, and let us assume that all the 138 appointed electors cast their votes in favor of four US Presidential candidates, no two of whom were from one and the same state. (The real electors cast their votes in favor of five US Presidential candidates in the 1800 Election.) Further, let us assume that the electors formed seven groups as follows: The first group consisted of 69 electors, the second group consisted of 34 electors, and the other five groups consisted of seven electors each. Finally, let us assume that electors from the groups voted as follows: All the electors from the first group voted in favor of candidate A, and 35 of them also voted in favor of candidate B, whereas the other 34 also voted in favor of candidate C. All the electors from the second group voted in favor of candidates B and C by giving 34 votes to each of the two. All the electors from the third group voted in favor of candidate A, and one of them also voted in favor of candidate C, whereas the other six also voted in favor of candidate D. All the electors from each of the remaining four groups voted in favor of two candidates. Namely, all the electors from the fourth, fifth, sixth, and the seventh groups voted in favor of candidates B and C, C and D, A and D, and B and D, respectively.

Had the electors cast their votes according to this scheme, candidates A, B, and C would have received electoral votes from a majority of 83 electors each, whereas candidate D would have received 27 electoral votes. The following table illustrates the distribution of electoral votes among the candidates:

	Candidate A	Candidate B	Candidate C	Candidate D
Group 1	69	35	34	0
Group 2	0	34	34	0
Group 3	7	0	1	6
Group 4	0	7	7	0
Group 5	0	0	7	7
Group 6	7	0	0	7
Group 7	0	7	0	7
Total	**83**	**83**	**83**	**27**

If only one person voted for as President by the Electoral College was a recipient of electoral votes from a majority of all the appointed electors, this person *was* to be declared an elected US President. If only one of the two or one of the three recipients of electoral votes from majorities of all the appointed electors received the greatest number of electoral votes, this person also *was* to be declared an elected US President. In all other possible situations, electing a US President *devolved* upon the House of Representatives.

A special mechanism for voting in the House of Representatives *is* proposed in Article 2 of the US Constitution. According to this mechanism, each state *is* given only one vote despite its size. The mechanism *represents* a part of the compromise between the large and small states agreed to by the Constitutional Convention participants [2], [8], [10], [11]. The number of persons voted for as President in the

Electoral College who *were* eligible to be considered by the House of Representatives is specified in the article in the following two possible situations:

a) There were two or three recipients of the greatest number of electoral votes from majorities of all the appointed electors. (Certainly, these majorities of electors could represent different subsets of the set of all the appointed electors.) Then the House of Representatives *was* to choose a US President between (or among) them.

b) There were no recipients of electoral votes from a majority of all the appointed electors. Then a US President *was* to be chosen from "... the five highest on the List ..." (of persons voted for as President by the Electoral College).

A US Vice President *was* to be chosen from the same list of challengers for the highest office in the country. Moreover, a US Vice President *could* be elected only after a US President had been elected. In addition, an elected US Vice President *was* to be a recipient of the greatest number of electoral votes among the recipients of electoral votes remaining after electing a US President. It is clear that an elected US Vice President *could* be a recipient of electoral votes from more electors than the elected US President if the election was thrown into the US Congress [1].

It *could* happen that only one recipient of the greatest number of electoral votes from a majority of all the appointed electors would remain after the completion of the election of a US President in the House of Representatives. Then this person would, in fact, be elected to the office of US Vice President by the Electoral College and the House of Representatives. If two such recipients remained after electing a US President, the US Senate *was* to choose a US Vice President between them. Otherwise, the US Senate would elect a US Vice President among the recipients of electoral votes whose number *was not*, generally, limited to four (persons remaining on the above-mentioned "List" after the completion of the election of a US President).

Indeed, let us assume that the greatest number of electoral votes was received by only one person from less than a majority of all the appointed electors and that this person was elected to the office of US President by the House of Representatives. Further, let us assume that there were more than four recipients of one and the same number of electoral votes smaller than this greatest number. Then all these recipients of this smaller number of electoral votes, who were eligible to be among " ... the five highest on the List ... ," *were* to be considered by the US Senate in electing a US Vice President there. Finally, let us assume that four persons (the recipients of this smaller number of electoral votes) were selected to be "... on the List ..." (though no mechanism for selecting these four persons among more than four such persons was determined by Article 2 of the US Constitution). Then, besides these four persons, all the persons with the above-mentioned one and the same number of electoral votes would have been eligible to be considered by the US Senate in electing a US Vice President there after the completion of the election of a US President by the House or Representatives. The voting procedure in the US Senate *was* to be held by ballot, and each US Senator *is* to vote as an individual rather than according to the will of his or her state. According to Section 3 of Article 1 of the US Constitution, the acting US Vice President *could* break a tie in electing a US Vice President in the US Senate.

2. *Amendment 12 of the US Constitution: a major step in modifying the initial election system.*

The Twelfth Amendment left the three-level structure of the election system unchanged. However, the amendment substantially changed the manner in which the second and third levels of the initial system operate.

Namely, Amendment 12 of the US Constitution

a) introduced the principle of separately voting for President and for Vice President in the Electoral College and the principle of separately voting for President and for Vice President in a US Presidential election thrown into the US Congress,

b) reduced the number of persons voted for as President in the Electoral College to be considered by the House of Representatives if electing a US President were to be thrown into the US Congress,

c) limited the number of persons (voted for as Vice President in the Electoral College) to be considered by the US Senate if electing a US Vice President were to be thrown into the US Congress,

d) required that a US Vice President would be elected in the US Senate only by a majority of the whole number of US Senators and only if a quorum of at least two-thirds of all the US Senators voted for Vice President, and

e) allowed the US Senate to hold the election of a US Vice President there not necessarily by ballot.

Many scholars in the field believe that the introduction of the principle of separately voting for President and for Vice President in the Electoral College was caused by the electoral tie in the 1800 Election [2], [8], [10]. At the same time, the language employed in the Twelfth Amendment is such that, formally, this amendment may not cover the case of an electoral tie in the Electoral College [1]. Moreover, generally, the text of the amendment leaves it unclear how many persons voted for as President by the Electoral College are to be considered by the House of Representatives if electing a US President is thrown into the US Congress [1].

Let us assume that there is a tie in the Electoral College, for instance, between two recipients of one and the same number of electoral votes as President. Further, let us assume that the phrase "the highest numbers" is attributed to electoral votes received by these two persons (as scholars

17

in the field usually believe [8]). Then, formally, there are two persons having "the highest number" (one and the same) rather than two persons having "the highest numbers" of electoral votes. Thus, in order to cover the case of an electoral tie in the Electoral College, one should attribute the sense of singularity to the plural noun "numbers," which contradicts common sense.

Let us assume that the phrase "the highest numbers" could refer to positions " ...on the list of those voted for as President ..." [1], [5]. Then under certain assumptions about the procedure of compiling the list of persons voted for as President, the tie under consideration is covered by the Twelfth Amendment [1]. "Extreme Outcomes of US Presidential Elections" [1] and "An Elementary Analysis of Some Mathematical Concepts Employed in and Relations Associated with Amendment 12 of the U.S. Constitution" [12] provide a detailed analysis of the language employed in the Twelfth Amendment.

Further, let us assume that none of three persons voted for as President received a majority of the electoral votes that are in play in the election. In addition, let us assume that they received different numbers of electoral votes. Finally, let us assume that the phrase "... not exceeding three ..." from the amendment is attributed to the word "persons." Then one, two, or three persons meet the requirement of the amendment and can represent not more than three contestants in electing a US President in the House of Representatives. A sense close to the intuitive perception of the phrase "the highest numbers" can be attributed to this phrase [1]. Nevertheless, even in this case, it remains unclear whether only two persons should be viewed as those with the "highest numbers" among the three persons [1]. Possible relationships among the numbers of electoral votes that can be received by at least four persons in a US Presidential election are considered in "Extreme Outcomes of US Presidential Elections" [1].

If at least four persons are eligible to be the contestants in electing a US President in the House of Representatives, the Twelfth Amendment does not provide a mechanism for selecting not more than three persons among them. Indeed, let us assume that at least four persons receive one and the same greatest number of electoral votes. Then it is unclear how not more than three persons to be considered by the House of Representatives can be selected among them. The same is true for selecting two persons voted for as Vice President in the Electoral College among at least three recipients of one and the same greatest number of electoral votes. Certainly, a problem similar to the first of these two problems existed under the initial double-balloting principle of voting for President, determined by Article 2 of the US Constitution.

The introduction of the principle of separately voting for President and for Vice President in the Electoral College made a difference in US Presidential elections. Situations in which a US President can be elected after a US Vice President has been elected, which were prohibited by Article 2 of the US Constitution, became possible. Let us assume that a person voted for as Vice President in the Electoral College receives a majority of all the electoral votes that are in play in the election. Also, let us assume that electing a US President is thrown into the House of Representatives and that this body elects a US President. Then a President-elect is a recipient of electoral votes from electors who do not constitute a majority of all the appointed electors. Under the election rules determined by Article 2 of the US Constitution, a Vice President-elect could not be a recipient of a majority of all the electoral votes that are in play in a US Presidential election if a President-elect did not receive electoral votes from a majority of all the appointed electors.

Also, the Twelfth Amendment for the first time provided for the case in which a new US President shall not have been elected to the office by inauguration day. Many scholars in the filed believe that Section 3 of Amendment 20 of the US Constitution superseded the sentence from the Twelfth Amendment containing this provision. Moreover, the same is asserted in a footnote to the text of the Twelfth Amendment of the US Constitution, which is published by the US Government Printing Office [5]. However, Chapter 3 argues that this assertion may be incorrect.

3. *The "winner-take-all" principle of choosing electors and the status of electors: a diversion from the compromise?*

According to Article 2 of the US Constitution, the legislature of a state directs the manner in which state electors are appointed in each US Presidential election. Nowadays, 48 states choose their electors by popular vote [6], [13]. The District of Columbia also adheres to this principle although the US Congress determines the manner of appointing electors there. Each person recognized as a US Presidential candidate in any of these 49 places (states and DC) is entitled to have a slate of electors there. The number of electors on this slate equals the number of electors that this place is entitled to in a particular US Presidential election. US voters vote for a slate of electors among all the slates participating in the election in the place. Moreover, currently, no US voter can vote for electors from different slates.

Although, formally, US voters vote for electors, a majority of the places (states and DC) currently use so-called "short ballots." Names of US Presidential and US Vice Presidential candidates rather than those of electors from their slates of electors appear on these ballots.

In each of the 48 states, the slate of electors that receives a plurality or a majority of votes statewide in November of the election year wins, and the slate of electors that receives a plurality or a majority of votes district-wide wins in DC. Electors forming the winning slate of electors are those who will represent the state or DC in the Electoral College.

The state of Maine and the state of Nebraska elect their electors in a different manner. The state of Maine elects two electors at large and one elector in each of its two congressional districts. The state of Nebraska elects two electors at large and one elector in each of its three congressional districts. An elector receiving a plurality or a majority of votes in a congressional district wins in this district. This elector is to be among the electors to represent the state in the Electoral College in the election. In each of these two states, two electors receiving a majority or a plurality of votes statewide win at large. These two electors are to be among those to represent the state in the Electoral College in the election as well [14], [15]. Both states use the short ballots in all their districts so that US voters in either state may believe that they vote for the corresponding pairs of the candidates. Nevertheless, formally, they vote for one elector in each congressional district and for two electors at large.

Only these two states can have electors that are to vote in favor of different pairs of US Presidential and US Vice Presidential candidates. There can be up to four pairs of US Presidential and Vice Presidential candidates who win electoral votes in Nebraska and up to three such pairs of the candidates in Maine. The following two examples illustrate this [1]:

Example 2. Let three US Presidential candidates receive 1600 votes total in the state of Maine, and let the distribution of these votes among them be as follows:

	District 1	District 2	Total (at large)
Candidate 1	**200**	300	500
Candidate 2	190	390	**580**
Candidate 3	110	**410**	520.

Then candidate 1 wins one electoral vote (in Congressional District 1), candidate 3 wins one electoral vote (in Congressional District 2), and candidate 2 wins two electoral votes (at large) although he or she does not win in any of the districts.

Example 3. Let 2000 votes be cast for four US Presidential candidates in the state of Nebraska. Then the following election outcome is possible [1]:

	District 1	District 2	District 3	Total (at large)
Candidate 1	125	200	350	**675**
Candidate 2	**200**	150	150	500
Candidate 3	50	**225**	100	375
Candidate 4	25	25	**400**	450.

Thus, candidate 2 wins one electoral vote (in Congressional District 1), candidate 3 wins one electoral vote (in Congressional District 2), candidate 4 wins one electoral vote (in Congressional District 3), and candidate 1 wins two electoral votes (at large) although he or she does not win in any of the districts.

The complete analysis of all possible election outcomes in these two states is presented in "Extreme Outcomes of US Presidential Elections" [1].

Thus, since 1969 in Maine and since 1991 in Nebraska, a pair of the candidates can win one or two electoral votes without winning in the whole state.

The status of electors has not been addressed in the US Constitution. Currently, there exist two viewpoints on the matter. Some scholars argue that the Founding Fathers reserved to electors the absolute freedom to vote their choice. According to the opposite viewpoint, electors were to express the will of those who appointed them. The US Supreme Court has several times rendered opinions relating to this issue. However, the Court has never addressed the issue itself directly [16], [17]. In addition, statements made by the Court in its decisions may seem to support both viewpoints.

For instance, in *Ray vs. Blair* [16], the text of the US Supreme Court decision contains the phrase "... even if ... promises of candidates for the electoral college are legally unenforceable because violative of an assumed constitutional freedom of the elector under the Constitution, Art II, 1., to vote as he may choose in the electoral college ... ." This phrase may, apparently, mean that the absolute freedom of an elector to vote his choice in the Electoral College at least should not be excluded as possible voting behavior of electors intended by the Founding Fathers. At the same time, in *McPerson vs. Blacker* [17], the US Supreme Court stated that "... experience soon demonstrated that, whether chosen by the legislatures or by popular suffrage on general ticket or in districts, they [electors] were so chosen simply to register the will of the appointing power in respect of a particular candidate ... ." This phrase seems to suggest that the above absolute freedom might not have been intended by the Founding Fathers (though this phrase refers to the practical implementation of ideas of the Constitutional Convention participants rather than to the ideas themselves). "Extreme Outcomes of US Presidential Elections" [1] provides a more detailed analysis of these and other statements made by the US Supreme Court in its opinions on the matter.

The discussion about the elector's status has been focused on these two viewpoints over the years. However, in "Extreme Outcomes of US Presidential Elections" [1], the author suggested another viewpoint, which cannot, apparently, be ruled out [1]. Namely, the Founding Fathers might not have been concerned about the elector's status and might purposely have left this issue unaddressed. For instance, they might have expected that new generations of Americans would reconsider the compromise that resulted in the creation of the Electoral College. Also, they might have believed that the new generations would propose a better election system or at least a better compromise on the matter. Moreover, they might have believed that the absence of a definitive status of electors would motivate a search for a new compromise or a new election system as the country developed.

No matter which of these three viewpoints may prevail under particular circumstances, the formal status of electors remains that of free agents [6].

Today, most US voters expect electors to vote in favor of the candidates whose slates of electors these electors represent. However, depending on the elector's status, such a manner of voting in the Electoral College may raise questions about whether the election system is in line with the compromise of 1787.

Under the compromise, neither the people directly nor the states are supposed to elect a US President at the first of two possible attempts to do it. The Founding Fathers believed that only electors, who apparently were supposed to be the most distinguished individuals in the nation [8], could exercise the first attempt. Electors could, eventually, elect a US President based on their knowledge, judgement, etc., no matter how they themselves were to be chosen. Electors were to vote in their respective states on one and the same day to avoid any pressure that some of them could impose on others [8]. If they were to fail, the states could attempt to elect a US President in the House of Representatives. However, if the states were to elect a US President, each state would have one and the same voting power—one vote—despite the state's size.

Let us assume that electors must vote according to the will of their respective states, which most US voters expect them to do under the "winner-take-all" principle. Then the first attempt to elect a US President would, in fact, be exercised by the states, and at this first attempt, each state would have different voting power, reflecting its size. This would contradict the compromise.

One may, however, object that by following "... the will of the appointing power in respect of a particular candidate ..." [17], electors, nevertheless, exercise their free judgement [1]. Moreover, according to the opinion of the US Supreme Court in *Ray vs. Blair* [16], "... the Amendment does not prohibit an elector's announcing his choice beforehand... ." In addition, by upholding the vote cast by a faithless elector in the 1968 Election [6], the US Congress, in fact, confirmed that choices other than those announced beforehand may not be prohibited to electors.

4. *Electing a US President in the House of Representatives: the 1825 rules.*

The US Constitution sets only basic principles of electing a US President in the House of Representatives in the election thrown into the US Congress. Therefore, the House of Representatives is entitled to set its own rules concerning the voting procedure there [6]. As such rules are not part of the US Constitution, each newly elected House of Representatives can either change already accepted rules or follow these rules. The rules of electing a US President in the House of Representatives were set by this Chamber of the US Congress in 1825 and have remained unchanged ever since [6], [18].

Article 2 of the US Constitution does not provide for a situation in which a US President is not elected in the House of Representatives in an election thrown into the US Congress. Moreover, the article prohibits electing a new US Vice President until a US President has been elected.

On the contrary, Amendment 12 of the US Constitution provides for the case when a US President shall not have been elected by a particular time. Therefore, the Twelfth Amendment makes, in fact, the option of not electing a US President a possible outcome of the election in the House of Representatives. At the same time, the rules of 1825 seem to eliminate such an option.

According to these rules, "... in case neither of those persons shall receive the votes of a majority of all the States on the first ballot, the House shall continue to ballot for a President, without interruption by other business, until a President be chosen." [6], [18] Moreover, Amendment 20 of the US Constitution, which was ratified in 1933, also provides for the case in which a US President shall not have been elected by a particular time. This amendment reconfirms that not electing a US President in the House of Representatives can be an outcome of the voting procedure there. Formally, the rules of 1825 do not require that electing a US President in the House of Representatives must necessarily result in choosing a person voted for as President to fill the office of US President. Nevertheless, it is hard to imagine that the House of Representatives will vote for President "... without interruption by other business ... " through the next US Presidential election if there is a quorum to start the voting procedure there as the option to adjourn can eventually be used.

5. *Conceptions and basic principles of the existing election system.*

Article 2 of the US Constitution reflects the following three basic ideas underlying the creation of the Electoral College [1]:

1) To have fair representation of the states in US Presidential elections. The Constitutional Convention participants believed that the states should be represented in these elections in the same manner in which the states are represented in the US Congress.

2) To delegate the very process of electing a US President and a US Vice President to electors. Each elector was to be chosen in the state of his residence "... in such Manner as the Legislature thereof may direct, ..." [5].

3) To recognize

a) the first choice of electors among persons voted for as President by the Electoral College as a US President if only one such person has received the greatest number of electoral votes cast by a majority of all the appointed electors, and

b) the second choice of electors, i.e., the first choice of electors among the residual persons voted for as President by the Electoral College, as a US Vice President if only one person among the residual persons has received the greatest number of electoral votes,

or to further delegate choosing either executive or both of them to the US Congress if electors were to fail to choose them.

Article 2 of the US Constitution stipulates the rules to adhere to in electing either executive or both of them in the US Congress.

The principle of unequally dividing the election power among the states and a manner of allocating blocs of electors to the states incorporated the first basic idea, to have fair representation, into the election system. The double-balloting principle of voting in the Electoral College and special schemes of voting in the House of Representatives and in the US Senate incorporated the third basic idea into the system. According to the double-balloting principle, each elector had to cast two undifferentiated votes for two persons as President in a US Presidential election. If electors could not elect a US President, the House of Representatives was to do it according to a special scheme of voting (see the explanation of this scheme earlier in this chapter). If the US Senate were to elect a US Vice President, another special scheme of voting in the US Senate was to be applied (see the explanation of this scheme earlier in this chapter). Both schemes were determined by Article 2 of the US Constitution for an election thrown into the US Congress. However, as mentioned earlier, no uniform manner in which electors should vote was proposed in the US Constitution for implementing the second basic idea.

The Twelfth Amendment has substantially modified the third basic idea of the Founding Fathers by introducing the principles of voting for a US President and for a US Vice President separately both in the Electoral College and in the US Congress. Also, the amendment has eliminated the participation of the House of Representatives in electing a US Vice President. As shown earlier in this chapter, such participation was possible under Article 2 of the US Constitution. Besides that, the Twelfth Amendment made possible the emergence of an acting rather than an elected US President for a certain period of time, as a result of a US Presidential election. Such an election outcome also reflects a substantial change in the original design of the election system today.

Thus, only the following original ideas of the Founding Fathers are present in the election system today:

a) The principle of unequally dividing the election power among the states by allocating blocs of electors to the states with the sizes of the blocs dependent on the sizes of the states.

b) A particular manner of forming these blocs of electors (or quotas of electoral votes) based on the distribution of the US population among the states. This idea is present in the system, along with Amendment 23 of the US Constitution (proposed and ratified later), which determines the number of electors for the District of Columbia.

c) The idea of giving the power to elect a US President and a US Vice President to three groups of people rather than to the American electorate. First, the power to elect both executives is given to electors, the first group of people, appointed in a certain manner by the states of their residence (and by DC since the ratification of Amendment 23 of the US Constitution). If according to the electoral vote tally, the US Congress concludes that electors have failed to elect a US President, the power to elect a US President is given to the House of Representatives, the second group of people.

If electors fail to elect a US Vice President, the power to do it is given to the US Senate, the third group of people (however, under circumstances not coinciding with those originally reflected in Article 2 of the US Constitution).

These three ideas of the Founding Fathers have been put to work together with the following new election principles introduced as the election system has evolved:

d) The "winner-take-all" principle of awarding electoral votes, a particular manner of choosing electors, introduced into the system under "... the influence of political parties ..." [13].

e) The principles of voting for a US President and for a US Vice President separately both in the Electoral College and in the US Congress. These principles replaced the double-balloting principle of voting in the Electoral College and the schemes of electing a US President and a US Vice President in the US Congress, which were originally designed by the Founding Fathers.

Throughout this book, the author employs a particular definition of a person elected to the office of US President, which is embedded in Amendment 12 of the US Constitution. Namely, a person voted for as President by the Electoral College is elected to the office of US President in the following cases:

1. This person is a recipient of a majority of all the electoral votes that are in play in the election. This is established as a result of counting electoral votes in the US Congress in the January that follows the election year.

2. This person is a recipient of a majority of state votes from (currently 50) state delegations if the election of a US President is thrown into the US Congress. This is established by tallying the votes in the House of Representatives (which happens in the January that follows the election year).

This definition is referred to as the first conception of the election system [1].

Article 2 and Amendment 23 of the US Constitution determine formal procedures by which quotas of electoral votes are assigned, respectively, to the states and to DC. Throughout the book, these procedures are referred to as the second conception of the existing election system [1].

In addition, in this book, the following principles of the election system are referred to as the basic ones [1]:

–the "winner-take-all" principle of awarding electoral votes in the states (currently employed in 48 states) and in the District of Columbia (DC),

–the principle of awarding electoral votes in the congressional districts and at large in the states of Maine and Nebraska,

–the principle of voting for a US President and for a US Vice President separately both in the Electoral College and in the US Congress, and

–the rules of 1825, determining how the voting procedure is held in electing a US President in the House of Representatives.

6. *Assumptions about the election system commonly believed by US voters.*

The US Constitution does not address certain issues relating to the voting behavior of electors in the Electoral College. Nor does it address issues relating to nominating US Presidential and Vice Presidential candidates. Nevertheless, many US voters believe that the following assumptions always hold in US Presidential elections:

a) US voters always vote in every state and in DC "... on the Tuesday next after the first Monday in the month of November ..." [1] of the election year. The voter turnouts in each state and in DC are sufficient to consider it legitimate to appoint electors according to the popular vote there. (The electors of) one US Presidential and one US Vice Presidential candidate from each of at least two major political parties participate in the election on election day.

As mentioned earlier, formally, US voters vote for slates of electors submitted by the pairs of US Presidential and US Vice Presidential candidates rather than for the candidates themselves. In addition, replacements of the candidates from both major political parties before election day are possible. Both US major political parties have declared rules governing such replacements under certain circumstances. However, the US Constitution does not address the issue, and this was indicated, in particular, by President Lyndon Johnson in his message to the US Congress laid before the US Senate on January 20, 1966.

b) On the first Monday after the second Wednesday in December of the election year, each elector casts two ballots. One such ballot is recognizable as a vote in favor of a person as President, and the other is recognizable as a vote in favor of a person as Vice President. At least one of these two persons is not "... an inhabitant of the same state..." [5] with the elector.

c) Persons voted for as President or as Vice President by the Electoral College are persons in favor of whom electors cast at least one electoral vote.

d) The voting procedure in the Electoral College results in electing a US President and a US Vice President. If unsuccessful, there is always a quorum to hold the voting procedures in the House of Representatives and in the US Senate. These voting procedures result in electing a US President and a US Vice President by the corresponding Chambers of the US Congress. If the voting is still unsuccessful, the persons to fill the offices of US President and US Vice President can always be determined according to Amendments 20 and 25 of the US Constitution and statutory provisions for Presidential selection. These provisions can be either those in force or new ones to be introduced by the US Congress [6].

Under these assumptions, the existing election system guarantees that two eligible US citizens will fill the offices of US President and US Vice President as a result of a US Presidential election without run-off elections [1]. However, even under these assumptions, the existing system has a formal gap between its first and second levels. Namely, there is no constitutional guarantee that US Presidential and US Vice Presidential nominees whose electors form the Electoral College will be among persons in favor of whom the electors will vote. This means that *the role of US voters in US Presidential elections is limited.* The US Constitution allows them to choose *only electors in the places of their residence (states and DC).* Moreover, *they can play even this limited role only as long as "… the Legislature thereof…" directs that electors are chosen by popular vote in the places (states and DC)* [1].

Once electors have been chosen (elected), only they can then choose a US President and a US Vice President. As free agents [6], they may nominate whomever they want to be voted for as President and as Vice President. By putting the names of particular persons on the elector ballots, they can constitutionally *elect their own nominees to the offices of US President and US Vice President. All that is required is to give these nominees a majority of the votes of all electors.* Thus, *electors can elect whomever they want to the offices of US President and US Vice President* instead of US Presidential and US Vice Presidential candidates whose slates of electors won in the states and in DC. Even when US Presidential and US Vice Presidential candidates are those or are among those whom electors decide to vote in favor of, electors may change the status of the candidates. They are free to vote in favor of US Vice Presidential candidates as President and in favor of US Presidential candidates as Vice President. They are not even prohibited from voting in favor of one and the same person as President and as Vice President.

Once again, under the assumed status of free agents, attributed to electors by the US Constitution, electors are (apparently) free to exercise their judgment in any manner they want. This may happen despite the binding imposed on electors in some of the places (states and DC). (This binding is currently imposed in 24 states and in DC [6].) *Thus, although, formally, more than 180 million US voters* [19] *participate in one election process, namely, vote for slates of presidential electors, the decision on the election outcome is currently made by 1073 US citizens as a result of another election process.* Currently, 538 electors and 535 members of the US Congress determine the election outcome as a result of this other election process. *Constitutionally, the outcomes of these two election processes are not necessarily connected.*

Certainly, under the "winner-take-all" principle, situations in which electors do not follow the will of their states and DC are extreme. However, the existing election system does not exclude these extreme situations.

At first glance, this situation may seem illogical. However, *the participation of US voters in US Presidential elections in the states is no more than a particular form of choosing electors according to the directions of "... the Legislature thereof ..."* [5]. The compromise attained by the Founding Fathers does not imply that the will of the nation should matter in US Presidential elections. Moreover, even *the will of the states formally matters only when electors (chosen in any manner) fail to elect a US President.* This is why the "winner-take-all" principle seems to distort the initial idea of electors first electing a US President and US Vice President. Certainly, the distortion formally takes place if electors, who are elected according to the will of the states and DC, must follow this will.

The absence of a formal connection between outcomes of the two election processes may cause weird situations in US Presidential elections. These situations are among the subjects of consideration in this book. Moreover, extreme election outcomes may occur even if assumptions a)-d) cited on pages 30-32 hold, along with the assumption that electors vote in favor of only US Presidential candidates and US Vice Presidential candidates. These election outcomes are also discussed in the book. Finally, the omitting of some of these four assumptions, some combinations of these assumptions, or certain of their parts may cause additional extreme election outcomes. Chapter 2 discusses all these extreme election outcomes.

The existing election system may encourage the use of extreme strategies in the election campaigns [1]. These strategies are logically possible and are not prohibited constitutionally. However, these strategies may divert the election campaigns from their expected course. Moreover, employing these strategies may result in distorting the will of the people, the states (and DC), and even electors in electing a US President and a US Vice President. Chapter 3 discusses these extreme election strategies.

The author would like to make it clear, that throughout the book, he considers extreme outcomes, extreme campaign strategies, and extreme election strategies only in the framework of the logical analysis of the election system. To some readers, many (if not all) of these extreme election outcomes and strategies may seem implausible and even artificially designed. However, the detection and analysis of these outcomes and strategies may help US voters better understand the boundaries within which the election system operates [1] and better comprehend their choice on election day. In addition, the analysis of extreme election outcomes and strategies may, eventually, contribute to improving the election system and will undoubtedly arm the readers with knowledge about the system. This knowledge will help them understand discussions of US Presidential elections and even encourage them to participate in these discussions in person.

7. Some additional principles of the election system.

Besides basic principles of the election system, the US Constitution determines specific rules of US Presidential elections. These election rules reflect developments of the system that have taken place over the years, and they embody certain principles of the system. Some of these rules have further diverted the election system from its initial design.

Amendment 20 of the US Constitution reconfirmed that a US President may be chosen after electing a US Vice President (which first was established by the Twelfth Amendment). The Twentieth Amendment also provides for certain situations in which a US President shall not have been elected at least by the beginning of the new Presidential term. Article 2 of the US Constitution provided for certain situations in which an elected US President could not "... discharge the Powers and Duties of the said Office, ..." [5]. However, the article did not address situations in which both the Electoral College and the House of Representatives fail to elect a US President.

Amendment 22 of the US Constitution substantially changed the initial design of the election system. This amendment limited the right of an eligible US citizen to be elected to the office of US President. Certain limitations on the length of the term of a US President in the office were proposed in the course of the Constitutional Convention [8]. However, no limitations on the eligibility of US citizens to be elected to the office of US President were imposed by the Constitutional Convention participants. The Amendment 22 limitations may, in fact, be viewed as a punishment for being elected to the office of US President more than once due to success in governing the country (despite understandable motives underlying the amendment).

35

Some amendments to the US Constitution eliminated certain election restrictions imposed by the Constitutional Convention participants. For instance, Amendment 19 prohibited the abridgment of the right to vote based on sex, and Amendment 26 prohibited the abridgment of this right for US voters who have attained the age of 18. The US Constitution determined the rules to be applied in situations caused by unexpected decisions that can be made by a President-elect and a Vice-President-elect such as resignation before inaguration day. It also authorized the US Congress to provide for situations that may occur in the elections under certain tragic circumstances. The readers interested in studying such situations are referred to the book "After the People Vote: a Guide to the Electoral College" [6].

Chapter 2

Extreme election outcomes: who is at fault?

Certain components of the existing election system may engender at least sixteen extreme outcomes in US Presidential elections.

The principle of unequally dividing the election power among the states by allocating quotas of electors.

This principle may engender an extreme election outcome of the following kind:

Extreme outcome 1. A US Presidential candidate wins by a tiny plurality of votes in each state of only a small group of populous states that control at least 270 electoral votes combined. For instance, he or she wins in each of the 11 most populous states in the US Presidential election [1] and is elected to the office of US President.

Let us assume that only majorities of US voters constituting less than 30% of all eligible US voters combined, from each of the 11 states, vote in favor of (the electors of) the candidate. (Currently, this may happen, since approximately 56% of the US voting-age population reside in the 11 states [19].) Further, let us assume that the rest of US voters vote in favor of (the electors of) another (one and the same) candidate under the 100% nationwide voter turnout. Then the election system will elect the first candidate to the office of US President even if more than 70% of all eligible US voters unanimously vote in favor of (the electors of) this other candidate.

Such a possibility raises concern regarding the manner in which US Presidential candidates may structure their election campaigns. Some or all of them may concentrate their campaigns in a group of populous states which control more than half of all the electoral votes that are in play in a US Presidential election. If this happens, the will of the residual states and DC, as well as the will of US voters residing in them, may become irrelevant in the election. For instance, Bill Clinton won by a plurality or a majority of votes in each of the same 16 large and medium states in the 1992 and 1996 Elections [1]. (He carried California, New York, Pennsylvania, Illinois, Ohio, Michigan, New Jersey, Massachusetts, Missouri, Washington, Minnesota, Maryland, West Virginia, Tennessee, Connecticut, and Arkansas twice, along with some other states and DC.) These 16 states controlled 270 electoral votes in both elections, and they represent only 31.37% of the places (states and DC) forming the Union. Had he concentrated his campaigns only in these 16 states, both the participation of US voters from the rest of the country and the will of the 34 residual states and DC could have been irrelevant in these two elections.

The decisive percentages of US voters in the 16 states constituted only 25.26% and 28.54% of the nationwide popular vote in the 1992 and 1996 Elections, respectively [1]. The "victorious" percentage of US voters can, eventually, be reduced even more. For instance, a US Presidential candidate can win elections with as little as 12.48% of the nationwide popular vote if the number of the candidates who receive comparable numbers of votes exceeds three [1].

One may assume that certain relatively small "victorious" groups (blocs) of states, each of which (group) controls at least 270 electoral votes combined, may support certain US Presidential candidates. This may happen if the candidates claim to have particular features in their programs and past achievements and to possess certain qualities [1]. If confirmed by research, this phenomenon may change the course of the election campaigns in the years to come. One could then expect that future election campaigns of at least some US Presidential candidates would be concentrated in such blocs of states.

Allocating quotas of electoral votes based on the distribution of the entire US population among the states.

Under the existing manner of allocating quotas of electoral votes, the same number of US voters may eventually control 18 electoral votes in Michigan and 54 electoral votes in California in a US Presidential election. This may happen as a result of a migration of the population throughout the country. The migration can lead to a substantial concentration of families with children under the age 18 and (legal and illegal) immigrants, for instance, in the state of California. Moreover, theoretically, this manner of allocating quotas of electoral votes may cause even more weird situations [1]. Namely, only a few states or even one large state, for instance, California may (theoretically) control at least half of all the electoral votes that are in play in a US Presidential election.

For instance, in the year 2001, 435 electoral votes were divided among 50 states based on the entire population of approximately 281.5 million people residing in the US (according to the results of the 2000 US census). If, say, 173.5 million people had resided in California at the time of the census, this state would have been entitled to 268 electoral votes according to the apportionment. Thus, this state would have controlled 270 electoral votes total (with the 2 "senatorial" electoral votes) and would have determined the election outcome in the 2004 and 2008 US Presidential elections. This would have happened independently of the participation of US voters from the other 49 states and DC in the elections in these years.

Interestingly, the state of California occupies a territory of 411,000 square kilometers, whereas Japan occupies a territory of 372,000 square kilometers with a population of approximately 127 million people. Thus, theoretically, such a concentration of the population in California could have been possible. Moreover, formally, this concentration is necessary only at the time of a particular census for only one state to determine the election outcome.

Certainly, California, New York, Texas, and Florida, the four largest states in the country, may eventually become the only four states to control the outcome of US Presidential elections. This may happen as a result of a migration of the US population. The voter turnout in California or in these four largest states can, nevertheless, be low in a particular US Presidential election. Therefore, the existing scheme of allocating quotas of electoral votes also contributes to the emergence of extreme outcome 1.

Delegating the first attempt to elect a US President and a US Vice President to a group of people appointed by the states of their residence (and by DC since the ratification of Amendment 23 of the US Constitution).

This idea creates the danger of electors, chosen according to the popular will, distorting the will of US voters.

Faithless electors [1].

If some electors vote faithlessly, the following five extreme election outcomes may emerge:

Extreme outcome 2. A US Presidential candidate representing a non-major political party or an independent one wins at least one electoral vote in the US Presidential election. None of the other participating candidates wins at least 270 electoral votes in the election. The candidate agrees to transfer these electoral votes (or this electoral vote) to a US Presidential candidate from a major political party.

The transferred votes (vote) may allow the candidate from a major party to be elected to the office of US President if

a) all the electors who are to vote in favor of this major party candidate cast their ballots faithfully,

b) the electors (elector) of the non-major party candidate vote (votes) faithlessly, in favor of the major party candidate,

c) no electoral votes are rejected by the US Congress in the course of their counting in the January that follows the election year, and

d) the total number of electoral votes cast in favor of this major party candidate is sufficient to win the election.

Extreme outcome 3. Three US Presidential candidates win less than 270 electoral votes each in the US Presidential election. For instance, they win 268, 150, and 120 electoral votes, respectively. Candidate 1 (with 268 electoral votes) also receives a majority of the nationwide popular vote and has support from majorities of at least 26 delegations in the House of Representatives. While the election is supposed to be thrown into the US Congress, candidates 2 and 3 block this course of the election by agreeing to a particular pair of the candidates to fill the offices of US President and US Vice President. Such a pair of the candidates can be formed out of these two candidates and their running-mates.

As a part of this agreement, all the electors of candidates 2 and 3 vote according to the instructions of their candidates and give the agreed upon pair 270 electoral votes in December of the election year. If this move is not objected to in the course of counting electoral votes in the US Congress, this pair of the candidates becomes elected to the offices.

Extreme outcome 4. Four US Presidential candidates, candidates 1–4, win 270, 265, 2, and 1 electoral votes, respectively, in the US Presidential election. Five electors among the electors of candidate 1 (with 270 electoral votes) vote faithlessly, in favor of candidate 2 and make this candidate the election winner in the Electoral College.

One of the faithlessly cast votes is rejected by the US Congress in the course of counting electoral votes, and the election is thrown into the US Congress. Candidate 3 (with 2 electoral votes) has support from majorities of at least 26 delegations in the House of Representatives and is elected to the office of US President.

Here, a particular interpretation of the phrase "the highest numbers" from the phrase "... from the persons having the highest numbers not exceeding three on the list of those voted for as President, the House of Representatives shall choose immediately, by ballot, the President. ..." [5] is implied. Namely, it is implied that if there are at least three persons each of whom receives electoral votes as President from less than a majority of all the appointed electors, and no person receives electoral votes from such a majority, three persons always make it onto the list of those to be considered by the House of Representatives in electing a US President in the US Congress.

Extreme outcome 5. A US Vice Presidential candidate from political party A receives at least 270 electoral votes in the US Presidential election as a result of counting electoral votes in the US Congress. However, the election of a US President is thrown into the House of Representatives and results in electing a representative of political party B (or an independent candidate) to the office of US President. Moreover, the House of Representatives fails to elect a US President by inauguration day, and an acting rather than an elected US President emerges, according to Amendment 20 of the US Constitution.

Analogously, a US Presidential candidate from political party A receives at least 270 electoral votes in the US Presidential election as a result of counting electoral votes in the US Congress. However, electing a US Vice President is thrown into the US Senate and results in electing a representative of political party B (or an independent candidate) to the office of US Vice President.

Extreme outcome 6. A US Presidential election results in electing a US Vice Presidential candidate to the office of US President and in electing a US Presidential candidate to the office of US Vice President (in the Electoral College). This may take place if electors from a sufficient number of slates of electors vote faithlessly by changing the status of the candidates. (Such a change was made by one of the electors of M. Dukakis in the 1988 Election [1, 20].) The candidates from the pair formed in such a manner do not object, and no reason to reject such a switch is found in the course of counting electoral votes in the US Congress. Thus, this "switched pair" of the candidates is elected to the offices.

Also, electors may form the "winning pair" out of two US Presidential or out of two US Vice Presidential candidates. Let us assume that electors from a substantial number of the winning slates of electors decide to do so, the candidates do not object, and no formal reason to reject faithlessly cast electoral votes is found in the course of counting electoral votes in the US Congress. Then such a pair of the candidates is elected to the offices of US President and US Vice President. Moreover, theoretically, electors may elect to these offices such a pair of persons who did not have electors at all. If a majority of all the appointed electors make their decisions similar to that made by one of the electors of G. Ford in the 1976 Election, this election outcome may emerge. (This elector voted for Ronald Reagan as President though Ronald Reagan was then neither a US Presidential nor a US Vice Presidential nominee [21].)

The US Congress may not be able or willing to reject enough faithlessly cast electoral votes in order to block extreme election outcomes under consideration even when these votes decide the election outcome. Although "massive" faithlessness of electors has never been put to a test [6], according to the Federal Register, currently, electors from 24 states are not even formally bound by these states to vote in favor of particular US Presidential and US Vice Presidential nominees in US Presidential elections [6]. They may eventually decide not to vote in favor of those US Presidential candidates who head the winning slates of electors in their states. Electors from these 24 states currently constitute 257 out of 538 electors who can be appointed in all the 51 places (states and DC). In addition, the US Supreme Court may not find a reason to interfere in the election to block extreme election outcomes under consideration [1].

Finally, the vote of a faithless elector cast in the 1968 Election was upheld by the US Congress. Therefore, currently, the ability of the US Congress to reject faithlessly cast votes seems to be rather limited.

Abstaining electors [1].

When the Electoral College voted in December 2000, one elector of A. Gore abstained [1] by casting blank ballots for President and Vice President. This manner of voting in the Electoral College was not, nevertheless, considered a violation of the US Constitution. Moreover, this manner of voting may even meet the requirements of the Twelfth Amendment.

This may be the case if an elector casts a ballot though this ballot cannot be recognized as a vote in favor of any person. The ballot cast blank may still be considered as a vote against all those whom an elector could have voted in favor of had this elector decided to do so. Such a viewpoint reflects a logically possible interpretation of the phrase "to vote for" [1]. It is important to emphasize that here, the abstention of an elector is understood as a vote that is physically cast. However, this vote is not cast in favor of any person whom this elector could have voted in favor of. In particular, it is not cast in favor of US Presidential and US Vice Presidential candidates whose slates of electors form the Electoral College.

This form of abstention seems to be a legitimate manner of voting in the Electoral College at least unless the US Supreme Court provides an interpretation of the phrase "to vote for."

The US Constitution may or may not allow electors to abstain in any manner. Therefore, the US Supreme Court may establish that the (assumed) constitutional freedom of electors to vote at their own discretion includes their freedom to abstain. Under such an interpretation of the phrase "to vote for," the following extreme election outcome is possible:

Extreme outcome 7. Two US Presidential candidates win 270 and 268 electoral votes, respectively, in the US Presidential election. However, one of the electors of the first candidate abstains by casting a ballot that cannot be recognized as a vote in favor of any person. Thus, neither candidate receives electoral votes from a majority of all the appointed electors as a result of counting electoral votes in the US Congress in the January that follows the election year. The election is thrown into the US Congress, and the House of Representatives elects the second candidate (with 268 electoral votes) to the office of US President. This may happen even if the first candidate received a majority of the popular vote nationwide, and his or her electors received majorities of the popular vote from each place from a majority of the 51 places (states and DC).

45

Formally, abstaining electors are faithless in a traditionally accepted sense. However, it seems reasonable to distinguish them from the other faithless electors as, *at least currently, the US Congress does not seem to have any means to counteract this phenomenon*. Indeed, the US Congress can at least try to reject certain electoral votes faithlessly cast in favor of somebody. Unlike this situation, no actions aimed, for instance, at reassigning electoral votes that were not cast in favor of any person seem reasonable and fair. The example of the 2000 Election is illustrative of the importance of this problem [1]. Had only two electors of G.W. Bush abstained in the 2000 Election, this election would have been thrown into the US Congress rather than being decided in the Electoral College.

Abstaining electors can even change the outcome of a US Presidential election that is to be thrown into the US Congress, and extreme election outcome 4 is illustrative of such a possibility. Let us assume that two electors of candidate 3 from the description of extreme outcome 4 abstain. Then the House of Representatives might vote for the candidates none of whom has enough support there.

Abstaining electors can also make a difference under a certain interpretation of the phrase from the Twelfth Amendment, presented in the description of extreme outcome 4. In the situation considered there, the abstention of the elector of candidate 4 could change the number of the candidates to participate in electing a US President in the US Congress.

Delegating the second attempt to elect a US President and a US Vice President to the US Congress if the Electoral College fails to elect either executive or both of them.

Formally, the result of voting in the Electoral College is not final even when there is a winner of the election there. Therefore, altering this result may take place in counting electoral votes in the

US Congress, as extreme outcome 4 shows. Moreover, when two (or more) US Presidential candidates receive the same number of electoral votes, the election results are hard to predict. They may eventually favor a US Presidential candidate who has the least support from both the states and US voters. The following five extreme election outcomes illustrate such possibilities:

Extreme outcome 8. Candidates 1 and 2, two out of four US Presidential candidates, win 2 electoral votes and 1 electoral vote, respectively, in the US Presidential election. Candidates 3 and 4 win 268 and 267 electoral votes, respectively. No agreements on transferring electoral votes among the candidates are reached prior to the day when the Electoral College votes. Finally, all electors cast their ballots faithfully so that the election is thrown into the US Congress. Candidate 1 (with two electoral votes) has support from majorities of at least 26 delegations in the House of Representatives. This candidate is elected to the office of US President even if Candidate 3 (with 268 electoral votes) receives a majority of the popular vote nationwide.

Here, a particular interpretation of the phrase "the highest numbers" from the phrase "... from the persons having the highest numbers not exceeding three on the list of those voted for as President, the House of Representatives shall choose immediately, by ballot, the President. ..." [5] is implied. Namely, it is implied that if there are at least three persons each of whom receives electoral votes as President from less than a majority of all the appointed electors, and no person receives electoral votes from a majority of all the appointed electors, three persons always make it onto the list of those to be considered by the House of Representatives in electing a US President in the US Congress.

Similar election outcomes may emerge if, for instance, up to five US Presidential candidates win only one electoral vote each. At least two such candidates may agree to combine "their" electoral votes. Let us assume that no agreements on transferring electoral votes are reached among the other US Presidential candidates who won electoral votes. Then this move of two US Presidential candidates with one electoral vote each may make one of them eligible to be considered by the House of Representatives in electing a US President there, and this candidate can even win the election thrown into the US Congress. This may become possible if no reasons to object to the combining of electoral votes are found in counting electoral votes in the US Congress, and this candidate has support from majorities of Representatives from each of at least 26 delegations in the House of Representatives[1].

Outcomes of the same kind may also take place if (two) winners of two electoral votes agree to combine "their" electoral votes. Two electoral votes can be won by a US Presidential candidate only in the states of Maine and Nebraska at large (see Chapter 1).

Extreme outcome 9. A US Presidential candidate wins up to 269 electoral votes in the US Presidential election, along with a majority of the popular vote nationwide. None of the other US Presidential candidates wins more electoral votes than this candidate. No agreements on transferring electoral votes among the candidates are reached prior to the day when the Electoral College votes. All electors cast their ballots faithfully so that the election is thrown into the US Congress. The candidate with 269 electoral votes does not have support from majorities of Representatives from each of at least 26 state delegations in the House of Representatives and is not elected to the office of US President.

Extreme outcome 10. At least five US Presidential candidates each representing a different political party win electoral votes that are in play in the US Presidential election. None of the candidates receives at least 270 electoral votes as a result of counting electoral votes in the

US Congress. The election is thrown into the US Congress, where each party has equal or close to equal numbers of seats in each delegation. The number of the candidates entitled to be considered by the House of Representatives in electing a US President there exceeds three. For instance, the candidates receive 132, 132, 132, 132, and 10 electoral votes, respectively, and there is no mechanism for selecting not more than three candidates among the four with 132 electoral votes [1].

Extreme outcome 11. Each of two US Presidential candidates wins half of all the electoral votes that are in play in a US Presidential election. One of the candidates receives a majority of the popular vote nationwide. The places (states and DC) in which this candidate wins electoral votes substantially outnumber the places in which the other candidate wins electoral votes. For instance, the electors of the candidate receive majorities of votes in 39 small and medium states and DC in the US Presidential election. All the electors cast their ballots faithfully, and the election is thrown into the US Congress, where the candidate with a minority of the popular vote nationwide is elected to the office of US President.

Extreme outcome 12. Electing both a US President and a US Vice President is thrown into the US Congress (see extreme outcomes 4, 7, 9, and 11). The elections there result in electing a US President and a US Vice President who do not represent the same political party. In addition, an acting US President rather than an elected one emerges according to Amendment 20 of the US Constitution.

The support of 26 delegations in the House of Representatives may turn out to be more valuable to a US Presidential candidate than a well-distributed support of US voters among the states. This may also engender the temptation to employ extreme campaign strategies aimed at throwing the election into the US Congress [1] (see also Chapter 4).

The "winner-take-all" principle of choosing electors in 48 states and DC.

This principle may substantially affect the outcome of a close US Presidential election. Winning popular votes by a US Presidential candidate from a non-major political party in a state or in DC may change the election outcome there. The following extreme election outcome illustrates this statement:

Extreme outcome 13. The electors of US Presidential candidates who do not represent major political parties receive small numbers of votes. These votes come from US voters in the states and DC who would have voted in favor of (the electors of) the candidates from major political parties if their favorites had not been in the race. (Many US voters believe that this was the case in the 2000 election although, generally, there exist US voters who will not vote at all if their favorites are not among nominated US Presidential candidates.) The received numbers of the popular votes are such that they change the election outcome for particular candidates from major political parties in the Electoral College.

A US Presidential candidate can be elected to the office of US President by minorities of US voters in every state and DC if these voters form pluralities of voters in the places controlling at least half of all the electoral votes that are in play in the election. This is illustrated by the following extreme election outcome:

Extreme outcome 14. The US Presidential election winner receives 538 (100% of the) electoral votes as a result of counting electoral votes in the US Congress. The electors of this candidate, however, receive pluralities of votes that do not exceed, say, 11% in each state and DC. (This can happen if (the electors of) at least ten US Presidential candidates are on the ballot in each state and DC.) The popular vote received by the election winner can always constitute less than 50% of all the votes cast in each state and DC if the number of US Presidential candidates (whose electors are) on the ballot exceeds two.

The principle of separately voting for President and for Vice President in the US Congress.

Extreme outcome 12 illustrates how this principle may affect the outcome of a US Presidential election thrown into the US Congress. Also, this principle equalizes the priorities of electing a US President and a US Vice President in the elections. Moreover, an acting rather than an elected US President may now emerge as a result of a US Presidential election, and Amendments 12 and 20 of the US Constitution determine how this may happen.

The intervention of US courts and the US Supreme Court in the election process in controversial situations may also cause extreme outcomes in US Presidential elections, which is illustrated by the following extreme election outcome:

Extreme outcome 15. The numbers of electoral votes that are won by the candidates in a US Presidential election do not reflect the popular will in some (or even in all the) places (states and DC). As a result, election outcomes in these places are contested by at least one of the candidates. Results of the recounts of votes cast in at least one of these places are also contested while these results change the election outcome. Such a change may make one of the US Presidential candidates the winner of the election even if he or she did not initially win the election. Also, the election that was initially won by one of the candidates may be thrown into the US Congress as a result of contesting elections in the places (states and DC).

Final decisions on awarding electoral votes in the places in which the election results are contested are made by the legislatures, who direct a manner of appointing electors [5]. These final decisions may also lead to the intervention of US courts or Supreme Courts in the states and DC. Moreover, even the US Supreme Court may get involved in resolving the disputes as it did in the 2000 Election.

All such final decisions lead to election outcomes that produce a great deal of controversy and disappointment in society. These outcomes can be viewed as extreme despite a) formal results of voting in the Electoral College, b) results of counting electoral votes in the US Congress, and c) results of voting in the House of Representatives and in the US Senate if the election of either or both executives is thrown into the US Congress.

Besides extreme outcome 1, the first part of the first conception of the existing election system (see Chapter 1) may cause the following additional extreme election outcome:

Extreme outcome 16. A US Presidential candidate who does not represent a major political party (or independent) wins the US Presidential election with at least 270 electoral votes. However, this candidate does not have enough (or even any) supporters in the US Congress with which to work.

Although electing such a US Presidential candidate to the office of US President is in line with the first conception of the election system (see Chapter 1), this election outcome may not be appreciated by society. Moreover, should this election outcome emerge, one could expect that the first part of this conception would be scrutinized.

Certainly, a particular perception of the (first) part of the first conception may vary. This perception substantially depends on how the concept of extreme outcome of a US Presidential election is construed. The perception of certain fundamentals of US democracy by both scholars in the field and US voters also matters.

Extreme outcome 16 illustrates a dependency on how the concept of extreme election outcome is construed. This outcome may seem extreme to US voters who associate particular expectations with results of US Presidential elections. Bills to be submitted and signed into US laws are among such expectations. At the same time, if this outcome occurred, it would demonstrate that real democracy exists in the US. Namely, the popular will (however, properly distributed among the states and DC) may prevail over the will of the political parties at election time.

If this outcome happened, it would indicate that a new political force is present in the country. An independent movement or a non-major political party, whose candidate wins the election, represents such a force. In addition, this election outcome would mean that (at least) a three-party rather than a two-party political system functions in the country at a particular historical period of time. The emergence of extreme outcome 16 could even be interpreted as a sign of, possibly, an improper representation of US voters in the US Congress through the existing two-party political system. Thus, this outcome may not be considered extreme by some US voters.

A similar conclusion about the above-mentioned representation can, apparently, be drawn under different circumstances. Let us assume that a non-major party or an independent movement is capable of throwing a US Presidential election into the US Congress. Then either political force at least deserves to be seriously considered [6].

The following statement illustrates the dependency of the perception under consideration on the perception of the fundamentals of US democracy: When the election is not won by a recipient of at least a plurality of the popular vote nationwide, the election outcome is always considered extreme by many US voters. However, the winning of the popular vote is not necessarily accompanied by the winning of the electoral vote in US Presidential elections [1].

Let less than 50% of all eligible US voters reside in the 11 most populous states, and let more than 50% of voters reside in the residual

40 places (states and DC) as a result of a migration of the US population after a particular census. Then these 11 states still control a majority of all the electoral votes that are in play in the US Presidential election. Further, let us assume that each voter casts his or her ballot in favor of (the electors of) one of two US Presidential candidates, and that all the cast ballots are recognized as votes. Finally, let us assume that

a) voter turnouts in the places (states and DC) represent the same percent of US voters residing in each place from the 11 states (group 1), and in each place from the residual 40 places (group 2),

b) majorities of US voters in each place in both groups represent the same percent of US voters voting in favor of the winning candidate in group 1 and in favor of his or her opponent in group 2, and

c) all electors cast their ballots faithfully.

Then one can be certain that under the existing scheme of awarding electoral votes, the electoral vote majority (accumulated in the 11 states) will never follow a popular vote majority in the election. A formal proof of this elementary assertion is contained in "An Elementary Analysis of Some Mathematical Concepts Employed in and Relations Associated with Amendment 12 of the U.S. Constitution" [12]. A numerical example illustrative of this assertion is presented in "Extreme Outcomes of US Presidential Elections" [1].

Thus, the existing election system can produce the above election outcome, and the ability to produce this outcome is an attribute of the system. Nevertheless, a particular perception of the fundamentals of US democracy causes many US voters to consider such an election outcome to be extreme.

All possible election outcomes considered in this chapter may seem extreme and even egregious to many readers. At the same time, some readers may not share this perception of considered outcomes and may raise a question concerning the value of describing these outcomes. In any case, one should bear in mind that the author considers extreme election outcomes in the framework of the logical analysis of the existing election system [1] and that the considered outcomes do not exhaust all such outcomes that the existing system may engender.

Explaining even the considered outcomes may help understand how the existing election system produces outcomes that US voters do not expect in US Presidential elections. Some of the considered extreme election outcomes can be eliminated while keeping conceptions and basic principles of the existing system unchanged. In addition, certain changes in the conceptions can eliminate the other extreme election outcomes considered in this chapter. Both options are discussed in Chapter 5.

Chapter 3

Stalemates in US Presidential elections: the danger of fuzzy election rules

When neither the election nor the selection of a US citizen to the office of US President is possible, a stalemate takes places in a US Presidential election. Stalemates in the elections are situations that cannot be resolved under election rules determined by the existing US Constitution and Federal Statues. Article 2 of the US Constitution turned out to be the first collection of rules for US Presidential elections that allowed the stalemates to occur.

1. *Election stalemates that could have been caused by provisions of Article 2 of the US Constitution.*

The requirement to choose a US President from "... the five highest on the List..." of persons voted for as President in the Electoral College might not have been met in US Presidential elections. This could have happened under the double-balloting principle of voting in the Electoral College if the election were to be thrown into the US Congress, and the number of electors was even.

For instance, only four such persons might have been available to choose from in the 1800 Election [1]. Each of these persons might have received 69 electoral votes, one-fourth of 276 electoral votes from all the 138 appointed electors. The requirement for each elector to vote for two persons, at least one of whom was not an inhabitant of the same state with the elector, would, nevertheless, have been met. Moreover, had the double-balloting principle of voting in the Electoral College been in force after 1804, the same situation might have occurred in each US Presidential election with an even number of all the appointed electors. Certainly, the above-mentioned requirement from Article 2 of the US Constitution is incorrect, and this requirement might not have been met in the 1792, 1796, and 1800 US Presidential elections.

Had only four persons received one-fourth of all electoral votes each in the 1792, 1796, and 1800 US Presidential elections, it would have formally meant a stalemate. Resolving such a stalemate would have required changing the language of Article 2 of the US Constitution.

Currently, the requirement under consideration presents mostly historical interest as it was superseded by provisions of the Twelfth Amendment [5]. At same time, this requirement remains a part of the text of the Supreme Law of the Land. This flaw in Article 2 of the US Constitution remained undetected for more than 200 years. (The author happened to be the first to notice this flaw and to analyze it in "Extreme Outcomes of US Presidential Elections" [1].)

In addition, Article 2 of the US Constitution does not provide for the case of failure to elect a US President both in the Electoral College and in the House of Representatives by inauguration day. Thus, at least theoretically, a stalemate of another kind was possible under the election rules set forth by Article 2 of the US Constitution.

2. Election stalemates that may emerge due to the failure to elect a US President and a US Vice President by inauguration day.

Can the election rules cause the failure to elect a US President and a US Vice President by inauguration day? The absence of the interpretation of the phrase "to vote for" from the Twelfth Amendment and the absence of any time limit for electing either executive in the US Congress can cause this.

One can certainly imagine a hypothetical situation in which a majority of all the appointed electors cast ballots that cannot be recognized as votes in favor of any person as President and in favor of any person as Vice President. (This is theoretically possible due to the current status of the electors and the absence of an interpretation by the US Supreme Court of the phrase "to vote for" from the Twelfth Amendment [20].) Also, one cannot rule out the exploiting of the filibuster to prevent the two-thirds quorums in both Chambers of the US Congress, required by the Twelfth Amendment [1]. Besides this, only political maneuvers by members of these Chambers may lead to the failure to elect both executives by inauguration day. The 1800 election in the House of Representatives represents an impressive example of such maneuvers.

The 1825 rules, which are currently in force, may also contribute to prolonging the election in the House of Representatives. According to these rules, a majority of each more than one-member state delegation must have voted for the same person to ascertain the state vote before the next balloting to be allowed to cast this vote [6].

The Twelfth Amendment requires electors to vote by ballot, which generally implies a secret vote. In 1800, Charles Pinckney, one of the Founding Fathers, said in the US Congress, "...To suffer them [the votes] to be known, as heretofore, has been the practice, is unconstitutional and dangerous, as goes to defeat in some measure, the wise provisions of the instrument, in declaring, that when the House of Representatives are to elect, that it shall be done, immediately. The Electors, therefore, ought to never divulge their votes … ."

Whether or not the requirement to vote by secret ballot should be considered constitutional, today, it is widely violated by almost all the members of the Electoral College. It is, however, the violation of this requirement that prevents the country from an egregious possibility of making only one pair of persons voted for as President and as Vice President recipients of the electoral votes from less than a majority of all the appointed electors. It is easy to develop an example of such an election outcome under secret voting by all the appointed electors to demonstrate how a particular pair of US Presidential and US Vice Presidential candidates could then be denied by their political opponents a chance to be elected even if this pair won a majority of all the electoral votes that are in play in the election [20].

It seems, however, interesting to analyze whether the above-mentioned theoretical but logically possible election outcome may lead to an election stalemate. Certainly, the requirement to choose a US President in the US Senate " … from the two highest numbers on the list …" from the Twelfth Amendment cannot be met in principle. Would electing a US President in the House of Representatives be possible in this case? This would depend on how the language of the Twelfth Amendment is construed.

The analysis of logically possible options to interpret this language is presented in "Extreme Outcomes of US Presidential Elections" [1]. This analysis shows that the requirement from the Twelfth Amendment " … from the persons having the highest numbers not exceeding three on the list of those voted for as President, the House of Representatives shall choose immediately, by ballot, President …" [5] may not be met under a) a conventional understanding of this language and b) the rules of 1825, governing the election of a US President in the House of Representatives.

According to the rules of 1825, in the case under consideration, the House of Representatives will have to choose a US President out of only one person. However, once the voting procedure there starts, this person must be chosen to fill the office of US President anyway. This seems to contradict the meaning of the verb "to choose," which implies that at least two options should be available to select from [1], [12]. Therefore, it seems that the election cannot be completed in the US Congress as neither of its Chambers can start the process of voting there. Thus, at the conclusion of the term of the acting US President, there will be neither an elected US President nor an elected US Vice President " ... to discharge the powers and duties of the office of President, ...," as the statutory provisions for selecting a US President address this issue [6].

No matter what causes the failure to elect both a US President and a US Vice President before inauguration day, one should bear in mind that there are no provisions in the US Constitution addressing this situation. Would it mean a stalemate should such a failure occur?

Only in five situations in which there is no one " ... to discharge the powers and duties of the office of President, ... ," the Presidential Succession Act directs a procedure to fill the office of US President. In addition, the phrase " ... or the manner in which one who is to act shall be selected, ..." in the text of Amendment 20 of the US Constitution seems to be attributed to the word "declaring" there. If this is the case, the amendment seems to authorize the US Congress to provide by law *only* " ... for the case wherein neither a President elect nor a Vice President elect shall have qualified ... ." Therefore, the act seems to be applicable only if either the Electoral College or the Electoral College and the US Congress elect at least one of the two executives. Moreover, a distinction between situations in which "... a President shall have not been chosen..." and "... a President-elect shall have failed to qualify..." seems to be present in the text of the amendment [12].

The Presidential Succession Act was enacted by the US Congress under the authority of Amendment 20 of the US Constitution [6]. Therefore, it is not clear how the act can be applicable in the case of failure to elect both a US President and a US Vice President in an election thrown into the US Congress. In this case, neither a President-elect nor a Vice President-elect exists. However, Amendment 20 of the US Constitution does not seem to authorize the US Congress to provide by law for such a case. Under these assumptions, Section 8 of Article 1 of the US Constitution might be the only basis to apply the act. In any case, only the US Supreme Court can decide whether the act is applicable when Amendment 20 of the US Constitution does not seem to authorize the US Congress to provide a remedy by law.

What happens if the US Supreme Court concludes that the Presidential Succession Act is not applicable in the case under consideration? Only Amendment 12 of the US Constitution could then govern the completion of the election. The Twelfth Amendment provides for the case of failure to elect a US President in the House of Representatives by inauguration day. However, it is not clear if the amendment provides for the case of failure to elect both a US President and a US Vice President in the US Congress (by inauguration day).

Let us assume that the phrase "the Vice-President" in the phrase " ... then the Vice-President shall act as President, as in the case of the death or other constitutional disability of the President. ..." [5] from the Twelfth Amendment can be attributed to the Vice President-elect only. Then the Twelfth Amendment does not provide for the case under consideration. Therefore, from 1787 through 1947, the country might not have been protected from election stalemates that could have been caused by the failure to elect both executives in US Presidential elections. Moreover, it remains unclear whether such a protection currently exists under the act.

Let us now assume that the Twelfth Amendment attributes the phrase "the Vice-President" to the acting Vice President only. Then the case of failure to elect both a US President and a US Vice President in the Electoral College and in the US Congress can be governed by the amendment. In this situation, Section 3 of Amendment 20 of the US Constitution becomes an election rule determining when a Vice President-elect can fill the office of US President. Certainly, such an assumption may seem implausible. However, this assumption would resolve the problem under consideration and might make the Presidential Succession Act less vulnerable [12].

Once again, only the US Supreme Court can decide how to interpret the text of Amendments 12 and 20 of the US Constitution. Analogously, only the US Supreme Court can decide whether the Presidential Succession Act is applicable when neither a President-elect nor a Vice President-elect exists by inauguration day. Until then, the stalemate under consideration cannot be ruled out, and this stalemate will cause a constitutional crisis in the country. The selection of the acting Vice President to the office of US President as an alternative to such a crisis may not be appreciated by the American electorate either.

Such logically possible situations may currently seem fantastic or remote from reality. However, one should remember that US Presidential elections represent the culmination of a political struggle in the country. Competing political forces may undertake all constitutionally allowable strategic moves in order to win the election *or at least to prevent the election of a particular candidate to the office of US President.* In any case, it seems reasonable to analyze the described situations preemptively. It is also important to publicly announce rules to be exercised in all the detected possible extreme situations in advance rather than after such situations occur.

Thus, *the Presidential Succession Act may cover more situations in US Presidential elections than those for which the US Constitution authorizes the US Congress to provide by law* [12]. Let us assume that this is the case and that the Twelfth Amendment attributes the phrase "the Vice-President" to the Vice President-elect only. Then *no corrections to the Presidential Succession Act would eliminate the considered possible stalemates in US Presidential elections.* Such an elimination can be done only in the framework of a new amendment to the US Constitution.

According to "After the People Vote: a Guide to the Electoral College" [6], the Presidential Succession Act is applicable in the case of failure to elect both a US President and a US Vice President in the election thrown into the US Congress. This seems to contradict the statement from the same book that the Twentieth Amendment cannot govern certain situations in the election when neither a President-elect nor a Vice President-elect exists and that only the Twelfth Amendment can govern these situations [6].

Theoretically, in a US Presidential election, voter turnouts in the states may be negligibly small. Also, the election may be boycotted by US voters in a particular state or in a group of states. Finally, US voters may vote against all (electors of) the US Presidential candidates. However, these situations and those of the failure to elect both executives in the Electoral College and in the US Congress are substantially different. Article 2 of the US Constitution imposes upon the legislature the responsibility of directing the manner of appointing electors in each state, and choosing electors by popular vote is only a particular method of appointing electors. Thus, *the participation of US voters in the election process does not matter from the viewpoint of holding US Presidential elections.*

On the contrary, the will of electors to vote in favor of particular persons in the Electoral College matters.

The Founding Fathers made US Presidential elections independent of the intention of US voters to vote and devolved the duty of the elections upon electors and the US Congress. This may favor the viewpoint that the absolute freedom of electors to vote their own choice could have been intended by the Founding Fathers.

Thus, should the House of Representatives and the US Senate fail to elect a US President and a US Vice President, respectively, by inauguration day due to any reason, an election stalemate may occur under the existing uncertainty about the applicability of the Presidential Succession Act in this case.

3. *Election stalemates associated with executing the Presidential Succession Act.*

Let us now assume that both a US President and a US Vice President have been chosen in a US Presidential election. Amendment 20 of the US Constitution authorizes the US Congress "... to provide by law ..." for situations in which neither the chosen US President nor the chosen US Vice President shall have qualified before the beginning of the next Presidential term. The Presidential Succession Act governs, in particular, the situation in this case. Namely, this Federal Statute determines the list of the US officers who may then act as President. However, the act can be applied only to "... such officers as are eligible to the office of President under the Constitution. ..." (see the text of the act, in particular, in "After the People Vote: a Guide to the Electoral College" [6]). At the same time, requirements that must be met by US citizens to be eligible for any of the offices listed in the act and those to be met to be eligible for the office of US President are different.

Let us assume that some persons from the list who could qualify as an acting US President are under either impeachment or disability.

Further, let us assume that the others from the list are not eligible for the office of US President in a US Presidential election. Then a stalemate may emerge as the election cannot be completed [12]. A similar stalemate may emerge when only one of the two executives is chosen in the election but fails to have qualified by inauguration day.

Logically, stalemates have had a chance to emerge in US Presidential elections. Currently, they may occur under certain fuzzy rules that determine the voting behavior of electors and the voting procedures in the US Congress. Certainly, these stalemates may seem to be remote or implausible. Nevertheless, it seems useful to identify and analyze them for the same reasons that extreme election outcomes are analyzed. In any case, eliminating the causes of possible stalemates would reduce the chances for run-offs in US Presidential elections.

In conclusion, fuzzy election rules embedded in the existing election system can cause stalemates in US Presidential elections so that keeping these rules as they are may lead to a constitutional crisis in the country. Certainly, the US Congress and the US Supreme Court could correct or clarify fuzzy election rules. As mentioned earlier, some of these rules can be taken care of in the framework of interpretations of provisions of the US Constitution determining these rules. In any case, it seems that the threat of stalemates in US Presidential elections should concern all the branches of the US Government.

Chapter 4

Three ways to win the US Presidency: which way to choose?

As discussed earlier, the US Constitution delegates the first attempt to elect a US President to the Electoral College and does not specify the manner in which an elector should vote in the Electoral College. Also, the US Constitution does not state that the Electoral College decision is the final say on the outcome of US Presidential elections. Finally, the US Constitution delegates the second attempt to elect a US President to the House of Representatives if the first attempt fails. This leads to three legitimate ways for an eligible US citizen to be elected to the office of US President.

1. *Receiving a majority of electoral votes that are in play in the election as a result of counting the votes in the US Congress.*

The American electorate usually expects the candidates from major political parties to try to win the popular vote in as many states as they can. However, formally, slates of electors are those who win popular votes in the states and DC, and each US Presidential candidate aims his or her election campaign at helping his or her electors win in November of the election year. In any case, the US Congress decides how many electoral votes will be received by the candidate in the election by counting electoral votes in the January that follows the election year. Therefore, the numbers of electoral votes that are won and that are received by each US Presidential candidate do not necessarily coincide.

Faithless and abstaining electors may cause a difference between the won and received electoral votes for a US Presidential candidate. Moreover, the (assumed) constitutional freedom of electors to vote their own choice may cause the emergence of new recipients of electoral votes. These new recipients may not be US Presidential candidates whose slates of electors were voted for on election day.

US Presidential candidates earn the right to be voted for in the Electoral College by helping electors forming their slates of electors win in November of the election year. However, electors have the potential to take this right away from US Presidential candidates [1]. Therefore, close attention should be paid by the American electorate to a possible redistribution of electoral votes that are won by electors of the candidates in November of the election year. Such a redistribution may take place both when the Electoral College votes and when electoral votes are counted in the US Congress.

For more than 200 years of the history of US Presidential elections, less than 0.05% of all appointed electors have so far been faithless [6]. The percentage of abstaining electors has been even less than that [21]. Finally, the US Congress has so far upheld the vote cast by a faithless elector only once. Thus, winning electoral votes from a majority of all the appointed electors in November of the election year seems to be a reliable way to be elected to the office of US President, and this way has so far been chosen by all US Presidential candidates since the first US Presidential election.

2. Receiving electoral votes from a majority of all the appointed electors by combining electoral votes that are won by at least two US Presidential candidates.

The (assumed) constitutional freedom of electors to vote their own choice can be exploited to accumulate a majority of all the electoral votes that are in play in the election. Extreme election outcome 3, presented in Chapter 2, is illustrative of how this may happen. The combining of electoral votes does not seem to be prohibited by the US Constitution, and such a course of action seems to have been expected in the 1968 Election [6].

In that election, a US Presidential candidate from a non-major political party could have made the candidate from a major political party the election winner. It could have happened had a major political party candidate not received electoral votes from electors who constituted a majority of all the appointed electors. However, Richard Nixon won a majority of all the electoral votes that were in play in the 1968 Election so that the combining of electoral votes has not been put to a test [6]. Also, electors who voted faithlessly in the past elections did not apparently do it as a result of negotiations of "their candidates" with the candidates whom these electors voted in favor of.

A similar combining of electoral votes may take place among at least two US Presidential candidates nominated by the same political party. Currently, each major political party nominates only one US Presidential candidate at its National Convention [22], [23]. However, as long as the US Constitution does not use the concepts of US Presidential and Vice Presidential candidates, nothing prohibits the parties from nominating more than one such candidate. Moreover, in certain past US Presidential elections, political parties nominated at least two US Presidential and at least two US Vice Presidential candidates [21], [1].

Such a political strategy has certain merits and deficiencies [1]. A particular political party may not have a candidate who could win electoral votes from a majority of all the appointed electors. However, one candidate of the party may have a good chance to win all the electoral votes in a part of any "victorious" group of the places (states and DC). If the other candidate can win all the electoral votes in the rest of the places in the group, this strategy may be reasonable.

What could be the reasons to exercise such a political strategy? First, the party's political platform may become more inclusive than it could have been otherwise. Second, the use of this strategy may reduce "political dirt" slung by the candidates from the same party to win the nomination. Third, this strategy may seem acceptable to US voters loyal to the party who will not vote if their favorite does not get the nomination. Fourth, those voters who have close positions on issues with different candidates from the party may also find this strategy acceptable. These US voters may even expect that two US Presidential nominees from the same party may ultimately be elected to the offices of US President and US Vice President. This seems to be possible due to the current status of electors.

At the same time, the nomination of more than one candidate by the same political party may cause this party to lose the votes of undecided voters. These voters may view such a move as the party's weakness on issues important to them. Therefore, this political strategy may become ineffective and even lead to defeat.

With the option for political parties to nominate more than one US Presidential candidate, the election system has the potential to change the very nature of the election process in the country [1]. Namely, a political party rather than a leader of the nation can win the election, and the winning party may then appoint such a leader. Certainly, if it happens, the appointee is likely to be a known political leader of the party. Moreover, most probably, this appointee will be a US Presidential candidate though, formally, this may not be the case. The decision of the US Supreme Court in *Ray vs. Blair* [16] states that the Twelfth Amendment does not prohibit electors from announcing their intention to vote for a particular party's nominee. Let us assume that this decision can be interpreted in a broad sense of voting in the Electoral College in favor of any party's nominee. Then this party's nominee can be, for instance, the one recommended by the party before the Electoral College votes. If this were the case, appointing a leader would become even more legitimate.

The above-mentioned change in the election process will probably seem unacceptable to a majority of US voters. However, according to the US Constitution, the nation does not, formally, elect its leader anyway. US voters residing in the states and DC elect only electors from their places of residence. These electors may eventually elect such a leader or throw the election into the US Congress. Should the US Congress elect a US President, the elected person may not be a leader of the nation in any customary sense.

Today, this political strategy may seem fantastic or even absurd. However, as mentioned earlier, this strategy has been employed in past US Presidential elections several times. For instance, the Whig party nominated three US Presidential candidates in the 1836 and 1860 Elections. The divided Democratic Party nominated two pairs of US Presidential and US Vice Presidential candidates in the 1860 Election. Nevertheless, in both elections, the parties which nominated more than one US Presidential candidate lost the election in the Electoral College. In both elections, their candidates received fewer electoral votes combined than the election winner.

In addition, practical implementation of this political strategy may present substantial financial and organizational difficulties. This may be the case even when the party puts only one candidate on the ballot in each place in which the candidate has the best chance to win all electoral votes.

3. *Winning US Presidential elections via the US Congress.*

The first conception of the election system, presented in Chapter 1, makes it clear that the US Presidency does not necessarily have to be won via the Electoral College. A recipient of a majority of votes from (currently the 50) state delegations may be elected to the office of US President in the US Congress.

Let as assume that a US Presidential candidate has support from at least 26 state delegations in the House of Representatives. Then this candidate may try to aim his or her election campaign at throwing the election into the US Congress instead of trying to win the US Presidency via the Electoral College. At first glance, such a strategy may seem unusual. However, this strategy may, eventually, be the only winning one for a US Presidential candidate in the election. This strategy can be implemented if the candidate can affect the election process and, possibly, the decisions of particular electors.

Let us now assume that there are at least three US Presidential candidates and that two of them have close chances to receive electoral votes from a majority of all the appointed electors. Then throwing the election into the US Congress can be viewed by the third US Presidential candidate as a reasonable strategy. Otherwise, the election will likely be either won by the leading candidate (or by one of the leading candidates) or thrown into the US Congress anyway.

How may the candidate attempt to throw the election into the US Congress? The "winner-take-all" principle of choosing electors may be exploited to this end. The candidate may be able to "switch" some US voters from one leading US Presidential candidate to another (or to the other) in certain places (states and DC). For instance, the so-called "swing voters" can be used to "balance" the total number of electoral votes to be received by each leading candidate. Certainly, such a total number should not constitute a majority of all the electoral votes that are in play in the election for any leading candidate.

How can the interested candidate find a "desirable" (to him or her) distribution of electoral votes to be received by the leading candidates? This can be determined based on the estimated chances of the other candidates both to effectively compete and to succeed in the corresponding places (states and DC) [20]. Once this determination has been made, the candidate's campaign can be structured to reach the "desirable" distribution.

By (indirectly) supporting the other US Presidential candidates in chosen places (states and DC), the candidate may attain the "desirable" distribution of electoral votes among the leading candidates and throw the election into the US Congress [20]. Supporting the other candidates can come in the form of debates aimed at weakening positions of the leading candidate in a state or DC in favor of his or her closest opponent there. Choosing potential candidates for the debates and the structure of the debates depend on political circumstances [1]. Certainly, the support should come in accordance with the targeted distribution of electoral votes. Appropriate advertising campaigns in the selected places aimed at defeating the leader there can be used to this end.

Throwing the election of a US President into the US Congress is only a necessary condition for winning the election in the House of Representatives by the candidate. This candidate must manage to make it onto the list of not more than three persons voted for as President in the Electoral College, who would be considered by the House of Representatives according to Amendment 12 of the US Constitution. This means that the candidate should receive at least a certain number of electoral votes as a result of counting electoral votes in the US Congress. Depending on a particular interpretation of the phrase "... from the persons having the highest numbers not exceeding three on the list of those voted for as President..." from Amendment 12 of the US Constitution, receiving either one or two electoral votes may be sufficient to make it onto the list.

Even if the candidate does not win enough electoral votes through the popular vote to make it onto the above-mentioned list, this manner of winning the election still may be open to him or her. The (assumed) constitutional freedom of electors to vote their own choice may, eventually, help this candidate accumulate the necessary number of electoral votes that are in play in the election. Moreover, theoretically, the candidate may win the election even if he or she did not win any electoral votes in November of the election year. No matter how egregious and fantastic this option may seem, it is logically possible [1].

Here, a particular interpretation of the phrase "the highest numbers" from the phrase "... from the persons having the highest numbers not exceeding three on the list of those voted for as President, the House of Representatives shall choose immediately, by ballot, the President. ..." [5] is implied. Namely, it is implied that if there are at least three persons each of whom receives electoral votes as President from less than a majority of all the appointed electors, and no person receives electoral votes from a majority of all the appointed electors, three persons always make it onto the list of those to be considered by the House of Representatives in electing a US President in the US Congress.

Finally, let us assume that the right of electors to abstain in any manner is confirmed by the US Supreme Court. Then extreme election outcome 4, presented in Chapter 2, suggests that an egregious election outcome may (theoretically) take place. A US Presidential candidate can win the election in the US Congress even if he or she did not win any electoral votes, despite the fact that one of the other candidates won electoral votes from a majority of all the appointed electors.

A political party may employ the strategy of winning the US Presidency in the US Congress by nominating more than one US Presidential candidate if the party controls majorities of at least 26 delegations in the House of Representatives. This strategy can be combined with the one described earlier in Section 2 of this chapter. Namely, the party may nominate more than one US Presidential candidate and try to win the election in the Electoral College. If this does not work, the party may try to throw the election into the US Congress and win the US Presidency in the House of Representatives. Certainly, corresponding adjustments in the campaign strategy would have to be made by the party in this case.

The described strategy may substantially divert the election campaign from its customary course. Certainly, a US Presidential candidate can choose the strategy to win the election via the Electoral College while bearing in mind the option to throw the election into the US Congress. However, this strategy substantially differs from the one aimed at throwing the election into the US Congress at the very beginning of the election campaign [1].

Chapter 5

To change or not to change: does the country really need a new election system?

Possible extreme outcomes and stalemates in US Presidential elections may raise concerns about the existing election system. Some readers may believe that the time for certain changes in the system has come. They may expect that the changes would eliminate the very possibility of emerging extreme situations in US Presidential elections. Some other readers may believe that an election system capable of engendering such extreme situations should be "punished" by replacing it with another one. (The direct popular election system is often viewed as an alternative to the existing one [8], [9].) Some readers may believe that the system that has successfully served the nation for more than two centuries should remain unchanged. Certainly, there may be some readers who do not care, especially those who do not vote in US Presidential elections. (Usually, more than 40% of US voters do not vote in US Presidential elections [19] so that this particular perception cannot, apparently, be ruled out.) Finally, some readers may believe that any changes in the system or of the system itself are practically impossible no matter how reasonable these changes could be.

The presented spectrum of possible perceptions of the election system seems to be in line with public opinion polls regarding abolishing the Electoral College. The Gallup polls conducted in February, April--May, and November 1967 show that 58%, 63%, and 65% of the respondents, respectively, were in favor of abolishing the Electoral College [8]. Public opinion polls held in 1968 and 1981 show that 81% and 75% of their participants, respectively, also were in favor of such an action [2].

Numerous modifications in the existing election system and variants of a new election system have been proposed for more than 200 years. Some of them were proposed by members of the US Government, especially by those of the US Senate in 1968–1970 [24]. In addition, in 1967, the American Bar Association recommended replacing the existing system with a direct popular election system of a particular kind. These recommendations were supported by the House of Representatives in 1969 and were close to gaining the support of the US Senate in 1970 [6]. Nevertheless, scholars and political leaders are not united on this matter. While many of them oppose the idea of changing the system [2], [13], [25], some others suggest that certain changes in the system should be considered [9].

What underlies public perceptions of the election system? To answer this question, first, one should find out what this system was created for. Second, one should comprehend to what extent the currently existing election system, designed more than 200 years ago and modified many times since then, can satisfactorily serve society today.

The initial system was designed as a tool for electing a Chief Executive to govern the Union of the states [1], [2], [8], [9], [25]. As a result of a compromise, the elected Chief Executive was not supposed to have a mandate from the American electorate. This mandate was to be given to the Chief Executive either by electors or by the states in the House of Representatives. *If electors were to fail to elect the Chief Executive, no run-offs in the Electoral College were allowed.* Instead, the assembly of the states as equal subjects of the Union would choose a Chief Executive in this case. The Constitutional Convention participants viewed this assembly as the ultimate appointing power in electing a US President.

Why did the Founding Fathers disallow the run-off elections in the Electoral College? They might have believed that the failure to elect a US President there would have manifested lack of agreement among electors on a leader to govern the Union at the time of holding the election. They might also have believed that no run-offs in the Electoral College could change the underlying intent of its members.

Changes that have been made in the election system since its creation have generated in US voters other views about the purposes of the system. Many of them believe that an elected US President should have a mandate directly from the American electorate. In addition, throwing the election into the US Congress is often viewed as a disaster [2]. Therefore, numerous attempts to change the system have focused on eliminating the election of a US President in the House of Representatives.

Artificially re-awarding electoral votes was proposed to replace the election of a Chief Executive in the US Congress. The idea of the replacement is always to elect a US President who is a recipient of at least a plurality of the nationwide popular vote [24]. Popular elections with run-offs have been proposed many times, despite the fact that such an election scheme can engender stalemates in US Presidential elections. Indeed, people who firmly commit to particular beliefs may not change their vote in the course of the run-offs. If that is the case, the run-offs become senseless [1].

The proposed changes bear evidence that the views of both scholars in the field and many US voters on the existing election system do not coincide with those of the Founding Fathers. At the same time, despite all the deficiencies of the existing election system, many US voters believe that this system has successfully served the nation for more than two centuries [1], [2], [9], [13], [25]. In any case, the discussion of the system usually emerges when the popular vote winner loses (or has a chance to lose) the election.

At first glance, one may expect that if the existing election system always elected recipients of at least a plurality of the nationwide popular vote to the office of US President, the results of the polls on abolishing the Electoral College would be different. However, even if that were the case, concerns of advocates of the principle "one man, one vote," which is not part of either the existing election system or many of its known modifications [26], [27], would remain unaddressed. These concerns are often referred to as being in line with the constitutional principle of equal protection, the key in deciding the 2000 Election outcome. In addition, if certain election rules remain as fuzzy as they are, they may affect outcomes of US Presidential elections in the years to come. Finally, the existing system seems to be too complicated to understand in depth, which may contribute to the unwillingness of many US voters to vote in US Presidential elections. Some of them may consider it unreasonable to vote as long as many election rules remain as unclear and exploitable as they are.

Thus, finding whether the election system should be changed in any manner or be replaced with a new one seems expedient. Three basic approaches to improving the existing election system that have been proposed over the more than 200 years since the creation of the Electoral College, should be analyzed to this end.

The first approach is based on the belief that conceptions and basic principles of the system should remain as they are. Some proponents of this approach believe that any changes in the fundamentals of the system may destabilize society. They also believe that those who push for the changes do not understand the danger of damaging the Federal system of government and representation in the US [13]. Some other proponents of the approach believe that necessary changes in the system can be made in a manner allowing one to avoid amending the US Constitution. Although beliefs of both kinds may seem reasonable, their substantiation is often unsatisfactory.

In particular, the following two beliefs, plausible at first glance, are widely spread [13]:

a) The Electoral College forces a winning US Presidential candidate to demonstrate "... both a sufficient popular support to govern as well as a sufficient distribution of that support to govern... ."

b) Without the Electoral College, US Presidents "... would be selected either through the domination of one populous region over the others or through the domination of large metropolitan areas over the rural ones... ."

However, the real situation seems to be contrary to these beliefs. The existing election system gives superiority (if not a monopoly) to a small group of populous states always to have a chance to decide the election outcome. The largest 11 states can serve as an example illustrative of this statement. This superiority takes place under any low voter turnout in these 11 states and despite any voter turnout and the will of US voters in the rest of the country. In addition, as shown in Chapter 2, the existing system may (theoretically) allow only one large state always to determine the election outcome. The analysis of other beliefs of this kind can be found in "Extreme Outcomes of US Presidential Elections" [1].

Although many such beliefs regarding the election system are not substantiated, this does not mean that these beliefs do not have grounds. At the same time, any statements that these beliefs are in line with attributes of the election system seem misleading and undermine the intentions of their authors.

Those who oppose these beliefs argue that the Federal system of government and representation in the US is based on the structure of the US Congress. This structure cannot be affected by changing the manner in which a US President is elected [1]. Moreover, those who advocate a direct popular presidential election system in the US may, apparently, refer to the Pledge of allegiance to the US Flag [28]. They may believe that the words "... One nation ... indivisible..." should be interpreted in favor of having *at least one representative in the Executive branch of the US Government with a mandate from the whole nation.* These people may also argue that the principles of the election system, designed by the Founding Fathers, were appropriate only at the time of their creation. They may submit that what was good for loosely associated states of free settlers cannot serve the integrated and unified American society. Although these arguments make sense, one should clarify what it means that an elected US President has a mandate from the whole nation.

It seems that one can speak about such a mandate only if the following two requirements are met: First, more than 50% of all eligible US voters should have voted in the election, and second, more than 50% of the voting US voters should have voted in favor of (currently, the electors of) the same US Presidential candidate [1].

In the framework of the first approach, the idea to introduce a direct popular election of a US President without abolishing the Electoral

College surfaced soon after the 2000 Election [29]. This idea is based on exploiting the right of the state legislature to choose a manner of appointing electors [5]. Namely, it is proposed that the states would award their electoral votes to the winner of the nationwide popular vote no matter how their voters voted. Let us assume that the legislatures of the states that control at least a majority of all the electoral votes that are in play in the election decide to form a pool of the states to act collectively in appointing their electors. Then these states may award this majority of electoral votes to the winner of the nationwide popular vote. Those who promote this idea believe that with such a pool of the states, no amendment to the US Constitution would be necessary always to elect a US President by popular vote as the Electoral College mechanism would formally remain in place.

If forming such a pool was constitutionally possible, this idea might seem promising at first glance. However, even if this were possible, it seems that choosing a US President according to the will of state legislatures forming the pool would further distort the ideas of the Founding Fathers.

First, according to Article 2 of the US Constitution, the state legislature is supposed to choose only the manner of appointing electors rather than to enter into agreements with other states of the Union on awarding electoral votes on behalf of its state. Moreover, the state legislature cannot force its will upon electors, who constitutionally still remain free agents [6]. Electors may not follow the instructions of the "appointing power" (the state legislature), especially if these instructions are not in line with the will of their (electors') voters.

Second, it seems confusing whom US voters residing in a state would be supposed to vote for. According to the US Constitution, they cannot vote for President and for Vice President directly. All they are currently allowed to do in US Presidential elections is to vote for electors of the candidates. What if the electors of US Presidential candidate A receive a majority of votes in a state, but candidate A loses to candidate B in the popular vote nationwide? If the state is a participant in the pool, its legislature will appoint the electors of candidate B to the Electoral College. As US voters voted for electors of the candidates rather than for the candidates themselves, this would distort the popular will of the state and would depreciate the value of the participation of the state voters in the election. Moreover, it would, in fact, substitute the will of the state legislature–which, in this case, would be declared in advance–for the expressed will of the voters of the state. However, one of the ideas of the Founding Fathers, underlying the 1787 compromise, was not to let the state legislatures elect a US President [8], [11].

Third, as long as the Electoral College remains, it may happen that all electors except for, for instance, one elector may be forced (by the pool of the state legislatures) to vote against the expressed will of US voters residing in their (electors') states. Indeed, for the sake of simplicity, let us assume that there are only two US Presidential candidates (A and B) whose electors receive votes in all the states and in the District of Columbia. Further, let us assume that all the 50 states and the District of Columbia are members of the pool. Also, let us assume that the electors of candidate A receive tiny majorities of the votes in all the 50 states and in the District of Columbia, whereas the elector of candidate B receives an overwhelming majority of votes in Congressional District 1 of the state of Maine. Finally, let this majority of votes in the district make candidate B the winner of a nationwide popular vote majority and give him or her all the (currently) 538 electoral votes from all the states and the District of Columbia. This happens despite the fact that the electors of candidate B lose the election to the electors of candidate A in each and every state (including the state of Maine in which the electors of candidate B lose to the electors of candidate A both in

Congressional District 2 and at large) and in DC. This seems illogical if not offensive towards US voters as long as they vote for electors of the candidates rather than for the candidates themselves, which still would be the case under the US Constitution.

Fourth, let us assume that at least two US Presidential candidates are tied in the nationwide popular vote and that the election results are contested. Further, let us assume that the disputes are not resolved six days prior to the day when the Electoral College votes. How controversial and frustrating would be either appointing "wrong" electors or throwing the election of a US President into the House of Representatives? This would be especially so if, for instance, one of the candidates wins 537 electoral votes from all the states and DC according to the will of US voters residing there, whereas the other wins the remaining electoral vote in a congressional district of, say, the state of Nebraska.

Fifth, under the "winner-take-all" principle of awarding electoral votes, the proposed idea would only amplify the already existing distortion of the intent of the Founding Fathers. Namely, the states with different voting power (which is the number of the state electoral votes) would still make the first attempt to elect a US President, whereas according to the US Constitution, the states can elect a US President only when a) electors have failed to elect a US President, and b) a US President is elected in the House of Representatives, and each state has one vote despite its size.

Sixth, although the US Constitution does not prohibit the states from forming pools, especially for commercial purposes, a "unified approach" of such pools to appointing electors may be found contradictory to the intent of the Founding Fathers. Indeed, it is widely believed that the requirement for electors to vote in their own states reflects the intent of the Founding Fathers to avoid "cabal and corruption" [8]. In addition, if not all the states joined the pool, forming such a pool could divide the country as deeply as ever before.

Seventh, let us assume that, say, five US Presidential candidates receive 21%, 19%, 20%, 20%, and 20% of the popular vote nationwide. Further, let us assume that the voter turnout constitutes, say, only 40% of the American electorate. Then it is unclear whether these 40% are sufficient to award electoral votes to the popular vote winner by legislatures of the states forming the pool, and what the legislatures would do if even the run-offs led to similar election results.

Thus, the whole idea to "outsmart ourselves" and to circumvent the US Constitution by substituting the will of a pool of the state legislatures for the popular will of, possibly, all the states seems perplexing to say the least. Certainly, constitutionally, the state legislatures have the right to appoint electors of their own choice, and the 1876 Election in Colorado illustrates that such a power of the state legislature can be deployed. However, one cannot disguise a nationwide popular election of a US President, which is not allowed by the US Constitution in any form, as a legitimate US Presidential election and appoint "appropriate" electors by a pool of the state legislatures based on the results of such a popular election. Also, one cannot have it both ways by asking US voters residing in a state to vote for the state electors and then appointing these electors against the expressed will of the voters. It may be difficult to persuade US voters to vote under such an "election rule" for the sake of avoiding the introduction of a new amendment to the US Constitution.

Moreover, this idea confuses the very goal of the US Constitution, which is " ... to form a more perfect Union ..." [5] rather than to outline a set of obstacles to be circumvented by the "ingenuity" of generations of Americans to come. Article 5 of the US Constitution states when and how the US Constitution should be amended. If more than one-third of the states do not want to change the system of electing a US President, one should understand the reason underlying their viewpoint and debate it rather than force any decision on the matter upon these states. No matter what new theories explaining the reasons underlying the creation of the Electoral College may be suggested in the years to come, it has been widely recognized that the idea of the Electoral College is part of the compromise between the small and large states that persuaded the small states to participate in the Union. Moreover, the "unfair" (as many scholars in the field believe) scheme of electing a US President in the House of Representatives seems to illustrate that the large states agreed to sacrifice their obvious power in US Presidential elections for the sake of forming the Union.

By signing the US Constitution, the large states pledged to honor the right of the small states to be treated as equal subjects of the Union in the final say in electing a US President. In addition, it is also believed that under the double-balloting scheme of voting in the Electoral College, electors were not expected always to elect a US President and that most of the time, a US President would be elected by the House of Representatives [8]. In addition, one should expect that if the forming of the pool was undertaken by some states, both the US Congress and the US Supreme Court might become involved. Indeed, this move may violate both the US Constitution and Federal Statutes relating to US Presidential elections, and, in any case, it may force the US Supreme Court to directly address the electors' status.

Finally, if at least three-fourths of the states supported the idea of forming a pool to circumvent the Electoral College, one could go ahead with an amendment to the US Constitution on the matter. Such an amendment could clean already detected discrepancies in the election rules and would "legalize" a direct popular election of a US President.

This would make sense if this scheme of electing a US President was supported by both the American people and the states as an acceptable modification of the existing election system.

The second approach is based on the belief that both conceptions and some basic principles of the election system can be changed though this may require changing the US Constitution.

Some proponents of this approach believe that the Electoral College as an assembly of people should remain in a modified election system. However, methods of choosing electors should be changed, and the so-called district plan and the proportional plan were proposed as such changes [2], [8], [9]. Some other proponents of this approach believe that the scheme of awarding electoral votes should be modified in such a manner that the winner of the nationwide popular vote would always win the electoral vote. The so-called bonus plan represents an attempt in this direction [2], [30]. One more group of proponents of the second approach concentrates on changing the procedure for electing a US President in the US Congress. Some even propose to replace this procedure with a run-off popular election if the Electoral College fails to elect a US President [2].

Finally, as mentioned earlier, many proponents of reforming the existing system propose to replace it with a direct popular presidential election system [9]. These proponents believe that such a replacement is what the country needs to make the process of electing a US President more transparent, more understandable, and more democratic. Certain merits and deficiencies of their plans have been analyzed and discussed, in particular, in [2], [9].

Among the plans to change the election system proposed in the framework of the second approach, one plan should be specifically mentioned. The so-called automatic plan, many times proposed, in particular, by political leaders [2], [9], [31], [32], consists of abolishing the office of elector while retaining all the other parts of the existing election system. The idea of the plan is to authorize the US Congress to count electoral votes that are won by US Presidential candidates by popular vote directly and to eliminate the procedure of casting electoral votes.

In "Extreme Outcomes of US Presidential Elections" [1], electoral votes to be awarded by the states and DC and to be counted by the US Congress in the January that follows the election year are called "pseudo-electoral votes." The scheme of awarding and counting "pseudo-electoral votes" is also described there [1].

The introduction of the automatic plan would eliminate an existing disparity between US voters and electors in expressing their will. Currently, a US voter may cast a vote in favor of only (the electors of) a pair of US Presidential and US Vice Presidential candidates among the pairs of the candidates on the national ticket. At the same time, a presidential elector may cast ballots for President and for Vice President in favor of the candidates from different such pairs. The introduction of the automatic plan would make this impossible. Electors, whom US voters give the right to vote for President on behalf of the state of their residence, would not be able to distort the will of the voters. In particular, introducing this plan would completely eliminate possible extreme election outcomes 2, 3, 4, 5, 6, and 7, presented in Chapter 2. Electing electors and electing a US President would never be two unconnected elections. Only US Presidential candidates would be persons to whom "pseudo-electoral votes" would be awarded. Finally, the first attempt to elect a US President on behalf of the states and DC would never devolve upon a group of only 538 US citizens.

At the same time, the US Constitution requires the election of a US President by the states to be consistent with the principle "one state, one vote." Therefore, the introduction of this plan would certainly change the original idea underlying the election system.

The third approach is based on the belief that certain parts of the old election system should remain attributes of the new one. Various plans, called hybrids [2], have been proposed in the framework of this approach since the ratification of the Twelfth Amendment [24]. Three plans proposed in 1970, which contain helpful ideas, should be specifically mentioned.

The so-called Federal System Plan was introduced by US Senators Tom Eagleton and Bob Dole. The plan proposes that a US Presidential candidate is elected to the office of US President if he or she is a recipient of a plurality of the popular vote nationwide, along with either a) pluralities of the popular vote in a majority of the states or b) pluralities of the popular vote in the states in which a majority of all the US voters voted in the election.

If such a US Presidential candidate does not exist, a recipient of a majority of all the electoral votes that are in play in the election is elected to the office of US President. Here, electoral votes are to be automatically awarded in the states and DC to the winner of the popular vote pluralities.

A recipient of an electoral vote majority may not exist in the election either. In this case, a US President is chosen out of only two recipients of electoral votes. One is the US Presidential candidate who received the greatest number of electoral votes. The other is the candidate who received the number of electoral votes either equal to the same greatest number or the closest to this greatest number. Electoral votes that were won by the other candidates are reassigned between these two electoral vote recipients. The reassignment is done in proportion to the percentages of the popular vote received by these two candidates in the states whose electoral votes are reassigned. One of these two candidates with the greatest number of electoral votes "received" in this manner is elected to the office of US President.

This plan incorporates both the automatic plan and the scheme of awarding electoral votes existing in the Electoral College. It abolishes electing a US President in the US Congress, the third level of the existing election system. The plan does not, however, address how only two candidates should be selected if more than two persons have won one and the same number of electoral votes. This plan also does not specify who is elected to the office of US President if the two candidates "receive" one and the same number of electoral votes as a result of the above-mentioned reassignment of electoral votes.

Another plan introduced by US Senator Bob Dole combines the automatic plan, the existing scheme of awarding electoral votes, and the nationwide popular vote in choosing a US President [24]. If a US Presidential candidate receives at least 50% of the popular vote in the election, this candidate is elected to the office of US President. Otherwise, as in the Federal System Plan, a recipient of a majority of all the electoral votes that are in play in the election is elected to the office. If neither such candidate exists, the US Congress elects a US President in a joint session. (A certain scheme for the participation of the District of Columbia is also proposed in the framework of this plan.) In this election, each member of the US Congress has one vote.

This plan does not address how many recipients of electoral votes out of more than two should be considered in electing a US President in the US Congress. In any case, the plan modifies the existing scheme of electing a US President in the US Congress.

A plan similar to Dole's was introduced by US Senator Bill Spong. This plan also combines the automatic plan, the existing scheme of awarding electoral votes, and the nationwide popular vote in choosing a US President [24]. A US Presidential candidate who receives a majority of all the electoral votes awarded in the election, along with a plurality of the popular vote nationwide, is elected to the office of US President. If such a candidate does not exist, the US Congress elects a US President in a joint session, where each member of the US Congress has one vote.

Like the Dole plan, this plan does not specify what US Presidential candidates should be considered in electing a US President in the US Congress. In any case, similar to the Dole plan, this plan modifies the existing scheme of electing a US President in the US Congress.

While these three approaches to improving the existing election system may seem to cover all the plans proposed so far, the author's approach, outlined in "Extreme Outcomes of US Presidential Elections" [1], produces a different plan. The idea of the author's approach consists of retaining the existing election system (with only two changes) while incorporating this system into a modified one. In the framework of this modified system, the nationwide popular vote can play a role in electing a US President. This role corresponds to a particular perception of society of who should be an elected US President.

In the framework of the author's approach, both the Electoral College mechanism for awarding "pseudo-electoral" votes, and the existing mechanism for electing a US President in the House of Representatives are considered protective mechanisms. These mechanisms guarantee electing a US President without run-off elections. Only the candidates who are recipients of at least a certain number of "pseudo-electoral" votes will be considered in electing a US President in the House of Representatives [1]. For instance, if three candidates receive 269, 267, and 2 "pseudo-electoral" votes, respectively, only the first two candidates will be considered by the House of Representatives.

The Electoral College may elect only a so-called compromise US Presidential candidate [1]. However, some US Presidential candidates may be perceived by society as better than or not worse than the compromise one. The modified election system gives priority to a better candidate and puts a candidate who is not worse than the compromise one in a contest with the compromise candidate (when a better candidate does not exist). Otherwise, the compromise candidate is elected to the office of US President. If even a compromise candidate does not exist, the House of Representatives elects a US President according to the existing rules.

According to the plan, a US Presidential candidate must be awarded at least a certain number of "pseudo-electoral votes" to be eligible to be considered by the House of Representatives. However, the receiving of this number of "pseudo-electoral votes" is required only if there are no candidates who are better than or not worse than the compromise candidate in the election. This number can be calculated by means of a simple formula [1].

Awarding "pseudo-electoral votes" rather than choosing members of the Electoral College is employed in the states and DC only if voter turnouts there are sufficient to consider this procedure legitimate. In all the states with negligibly small voter turnouts, electors are appointed as "... the Legislature thereof may direct..." [5]. Thus, both electoral votes from the places (states and DC) with negligible voter turnouts and "pseudo-electoral votes" from the rest of the places can be counted in the US Congress [1]. If no US Presidential candidate receives a majority of all the awarded "pseudo-electoral votes" and electoral votes cast by all the appointed electors, a US President is elected in the US Congress as directed by the Twelfth Amendment.

The society's perception of who should be an elected US President depends on several factors. The awareness of constitutional provisions underlying the election system, particular historical circumstances, emotional feelings about the country as a Union, and political propaganda are only a few such factors. Certainly, such a perception may not coincide with the currently assumed one. Thus, the compromise candidate, elected by the Electoral College, may not necessarily always be the best option for the country according to the society's perception. From the author's viewpoint, the people's perceptions of the matter are purely subjective and may be discussed only at the level of "my opinion versus your opinion." Examples of such possible perceptions, which, however, do not exhaust the totality of them, are presented in "Extreme Outcomes of US Presidential Elections" [1]. One should, however, bear in mind that detecting which perception currently exists in society may require holding nationwide referendums.

The author would like to concentrate the reader's attention on one such possible perception, to illustrate three conceptions of the US Presidency [1]. These conceptions may help better comprehend whether the existing election system should be changed or replaced with another one.

The first conception of the US Presidency is "President of the people." If a US Presidential candidate receives a majority of the popular vote nationwide, one may call him or her a "President of the people." At the same time, this majority should represent the will of the nation. Therefore, the voter turnout in the election should exceed 50% of all eligible US voters on election day.

The second conception is "President of the states." If a US Presidential candidate is a choice of a majority of the places (states and DC) as equal subjects of the Union, one may call him or her a "President of the states." This conception was, in fact, introduced by the Founding Fathers in the framework of the mechanism for electing a US President in the US Congress. Article 2 of the US Constitution determines this mechanism, and the rules of 1825 reflect its development by the US Congress.

No "winner-take-all" principle of awarding electoral votes in the states existed at the time of the Constitutional Convention. Therefore, the will of a state in the Union in electing a US President could be expressed only by its delegation in the House of Representatives. Moreover, this will could be manifested only if electing a US President was thrown into the US Congress. Today, the choice of a place (state or DC) can also be manifested in the form of a majority or a plurality of the statewide (and district-wide in DC) popular vote. The rules of 1825 require that a majority rather than a plurality of a greater than one-member state delegation in the House of Representatives ascertain the vote of the state in electing a US President there. Therefore, it seems logical to require that a "President of the states" elected according to the direct popular will of the places (states and DC) is a recipient of a majority of the popular vote in each of at least 26 places (states and DC). The second conception of the US Presidency considered in "Extreme Outcomes of US Presidential Elections" [1] incorporates this requirement.

The third conception is "President of an electoral majority in the Electoral College." This conception was introduced by the Founding Fathers in Article 2 of the Constitution and was later modified by the Twelfth Amendment. Currently, a "President of an electoral majority in the Electoral College" can be elected only according to the will of electors. If, however, a "President of an electoral majority in the Electoral College" was elected according to the direct popular will of the places (states and DC), the compromise candidate always would be a US Presidential candidate rather than any person picked by electors.

Proponents of the existing election system, apparently, imply that a "President of an electoral majority in the Electoral College" or a "President of the states" elected by the House of Representatives (if the former does not exist) always represents the country's best choice for the office of US President. However, American society may view it differently. For instance, US voters may believe that a US Presidential candidate who is both a "President of the people" and a "President of the states" according to the direct popular will of the places (states and DC) is a better choice for the country. Moreover, this perception may hold even when a "President of an electoral majority in the Electoral College" also exists. Extreme election outcome 1 from Chapter 2 shows that US Presidential candidates of both kinds can exist in a US Presidential election.

Other possible perceptions of society of which US Presidential candidate is a better (than the compromise) candidate are also possible. In particular, the American people may believe that a US Presidential candidate who is only a "President of the people" is always the best choice for the office of US President [1].

The modified election scheme, proposed in "Extreme Outcomes of US Presidential Elections" [1], works as follows:

1. "On the Tuesday next after the first Monday ..." [18] in the month of November of the election year, US voters vote for US Presidential and US Vice Presidential candidates in their (US voters') respective states and DC. Short ballots or similar voting schemes are used in the precincts. The states and DC certify the results of this voting (the popular vote distribution) in December of the election year. They either award "pseudo-electoral votes" to a pair of US Presidential and US Vice Presidential candidates in the manner in which the states choose electors, or appoint electors. The latter is done if the voter turnout in a state is negligibly small to award "pseudo-electoral votes" according to the will of the state. (As mentioned earlier, currently, 48 states and DC choose electors according to the "winner-take-all" principle, and the states of Maine and Nebraska do it by choosing electors in the congressional districts and at large.)

The US Congress tallies the (certified) popular vote received by the pairs of the candidates in the states and counts both the awarded "pseudo-electoral votes" and electoral votes (cast by the electors in the places with negligible voter turnout) in the January that follows the election year.

2. Case 1. The nationwide voter turnout does not exceed 50% of all eligible US voters in the election. Then the election outcome is determined according to the following existing election rules:

a) One pair of US Presidential and US Vice Presidential candidates receives a majority of all "pseudo-electoral votes" awarded by the states and DC (along with, possibly, votes cast by the electors). This pair of the candidates is elected to the offices of US President and US Vice President.

b) No pair of US Presidential and US Vice Presidential candidates receives such a majority. Then the election of both a US President and a US Vice President is thrown into the US Congress, which elects both executives as the Twelfth Amendment directs.

Case 2. The nationwide voter turnout exceeds 50% of all eligible US voters in the election. Then a pair of US Presidential and US Vice Presidential candidates may be chosen according to the people's perception of who should win the US Presidency.

One such perception may give priority to a US Presidential candidate with a majority of the nationwide popular vote and majorities of the popular vote in at least 26 places out of 51 places (states and DC). If such a US Presidential candidate exists, he or she is a "President of the people" according to the direct popular will of the nation. At the same time, this candidate is also a "President of the states" according to the direct popular will of the places (states and DC). Then this candidate is elected to the office of US President even if a "President of an electoral majority in the Electoral College" also exists in the election.

One may require that the voter turnout should exceed 50% of all eligible US voters residing in each of the above-mentioned 26 places (states and DC) to speak about a "President of the states" elected according to the will of the places (states and DC) [1]. However, the states may decide that this is not necessary and that a certain percentage of all eligible state votes can express the will of the state. The same is true regarding the District of Columbia, where such a decision can be made by the US Congress.

Thus, if the voter turnout does not exceed 50% of all eligible US voters, the existing election rules determine the election outcome. Namely, if there is a recipient of a majority of all the "pseudo-electoral votes" that are in play in the election (and, possibly, electoral votes cast in the places (states and DC) with negligible voter turnouts), there is a "President of an electoral majority in the Electoral College." This US Presidential candidate is elected to the office of US President. If there is no such US Presidential candidate, the House of Representatives elects a "President of the states" to the office of US President according to Amendment 12 of the US Constitution and the 1825 rules.

If the voter turnout exceeds 50% of all eligible US voters, but no US Presidential candidate is both a "President of the people" according to the direct popular will of the nation and a "President of the states" according to the direct popular will of the places (states and DC), the existing election rules determine the election outcome as well. It is important to bear in mind that the presented description of how the modified election system works reflects a particular possible perception of society of who should be elected to the office of US President. Some other perceptions of the kind may involve the consideration of both a better (than the compromise) candidate and a candidate who is not worse than the compromise candidate [1].

The difference between the existing and the proposed modified election system seems obvious even based on the considered particular example of the people's perception of who should win the US Presidency. The modified election system always gives preference to a US Presidential candidate who, according to the above-mentioned people's perception, is a better candidate than the compromise one. Only if a better candidate does not exist, or more than 50% of all eligible US voters do not vote in the election, does the existing election system take over.

Unlike the modified election system, the Electoral College *always refuses any candidates other than the compromise one.* This happens even if the compromise candidate is a choice of less than 30% of all eligible US voters from less than 30% of the places (states and DC). For instance, this happens even if 39 states and DC unanimously oppose this choice by voting in favor of another (one and the same) US Presidential candidate, which is illustrated by extreme election outcome 1 in Chapter 1.

Certainly, the existing election system can, eventually, elect to the office of US President a US Presidential candidate who is a "President of the people," a "President of the states," and a "President of an electoral majority in the Electoral College" according to the direct popular will of the nation and direct popular will of the places (states and DC), respectively. Examples of such election outcomes, for instance, in the last 50 years are well known [1]. However, the existing election system does not, generally, force US Presidential candidates to campaign throughout the country. Moreover, the existing election rules may make it reasonable to concentrate the election campaign in a relatively small bloc of "victorious states." (A bloc of the states is "victorious" if these states control at least a majority of all the electoral votes that are in play in the election.)

Interestingly, the modified election system and the existing election system would have produced different election outcomes in only a few US Presidential elections held in the last 50 years [1]. This would take place under certain possible perceptions of society of who should win the US Presidency that are different from the currently assumed perception. "Extreme Outcomes of US Presidential Elections" [1] provides examples of questions to ask in order to help detect society's current perception of the matter.

The proposed modified election system is presented in this book in the framework of the logical analysis of the existing election system. As mentioned in the Introduction, proposals to change the system could make sense only if there were criteria for comparing different election systems accepted by society. In any case, the proposed modified election system can be introduced only in the form of a new amendment to the US Constitution. The same is true regarding the plans that require more than just changes to the manner of choosing electors in the states. However, many new amendments to the US Constitution aimed at changing the existing election system have so far failed to be introduced [2], [6], [7], [24], [25], [26].

The proposed modified election system implies changing the first conception of the existing election system, described in Chapter 1. Without changing this conception, extreme election outcome 1, presented in Chapter 2, cannot be eliminated. At the same time, the including of the automatic plan in the existing election system would eliminate extreme election outcomes 2, 3, 4, 5, 6, and 7, presented in Chapter 2. Thus, these extreme election outcomes can be eliminated without changing the conceptions and basic principles of the existing election system (see Chapter 1).

The rationale presented in this chapter deals only with electing a US President. However, most of the proposals and plans mentioned here imply modifying corresponding election procedures for pairs of US Presidential and US Vice Presidential candidates. The same is true regarding the proposed modified election system. Approaches to choosing a US Vice President when US Presidential candidates should compete with the compromise candidate can easily be developed [1].

Some readers may believe that the proposed version of the modified election system is consistent with the third approach to improving the existing election system. However, from the author's viewpoint, this is not the case.

First, the modified election system does not require changing basic elements of the existing election system. ("Pseudo-electoral votes" and the formula for selecting candidates to participate in electing a US President in the House of Representatives are the only two exceptions.) Rather, it incorporates the existing system while allowing more options to choose an appropriate US Presidential candidate to the office of US President. Thus, the modified election system builds on the existing one rather than calls for abolishing the existing system or any of its parts.

Second, a better US Presidential candidate is the one preferred by all eligible US voters and by the places (states and DC) according to the direct popular will. One can consider that this will was expressed in favor of any US Presidential candidate only if more than 50% of all eligible US voters had voted in the election. If less than 50% of all eligible US voters vote, a majority of the American electorate either do not care or do not believe that (electors of) US Presidential candidates deserve the votes in a particular US Presidential election. In this case, one cannot speak about expressing the will of the nation with respect to (electors of) US Presidential candidates who receive the votes. Such requirements are not present, for instance, in the hybrid plans mentioned in this chapter.

Third, electoral votes are currently awarded in the states and DC according to the will of a plurality rather than necessarily a majority of the popular vote there. However, this may lead to undesirable election outcomes [1]. Therefore, majorities rather than pluralities of the popular vote in the places (states and DC) are required by the rules of the proposed modified election system in deciding whether the will of the places has been expressed in the election.

Fourth, a "mixed" form of representation is employed in the framework of the first attempt to elect a US President under the rules of the modified election system. Namely, equal representation of the American people reflecting their will is secured by the requirement that an elected US President is to be a "President of the people," whereas equal representation of states reflecting their will via statewide popular vote is secured by the requirement that an elected US President is to be a "President of the states."

Only if there is no person who is both a "President of the people" and a "President of the states" in a particular US Presidential election, the awarding of "pseudo-electoral" votes and, possibly, electoral votes (in the states with negligible voter turnout) constitutes the second attempt to elect a Chief Executive. If only "pseudo-electoral" votes are awarded, one can consider that a particular "mixed" form of representation of the states and the people is employed in the framework of this second attempt as well though neither the representation of the people nor the representation of states is equal. (The same form of (unequal) representation takes place in the Electoral College if all the electors from each state and DC are chosen by popular vote and follow the direct will of their voters.)

Should both attempts to elect a Chief Executive fail, a particular form of equal representation of the states, though not via the direct will of voters from each state, is used in electing a US President in the House of Representatives.

Finally, in the light of approaching the 220th anniversary of the Electoral College in 2007, a few words about the chances of the modified election system to be introduced and the impact that its introduction may have on American political life are in order.

Despite public opinion polls favoring the abolition of the Electoral College, mentioned at the beginning of this chapter, political pundits seem to be united in the belief that this political institution cannot be improved or abolished. Indeed, the equal suffrage of states in amending the US Constitution [2] discourages attempts to reform this election mechanism. Currently, 17 states with 5 and fewer electoral votes each are unlikely to sacrifice their right to eventually have a say in deciding the election outcome. This explains why proponents of abolishing the Electoral College in favor of a direct popular election, pushing small states to concede while offering them nothing in exchange, fail.

At the same time, a fairer treatment of small states may result in the favoring of the use of the "one man, one vote" principle—underlying all other elections in the country—in US Presidential elections by at least the three-fourths of state legislatures necessary to amend the US Constitution.

The modified election system allows a candidate with the nationwide popular vote majority and popular vote majorities in at least 26 states (or in 25 states and DC) to win the US Presidency even if somebody else wins the Electoral College. (Such a distribution of the popular vote and the electoral vote could have taken place in the 2004 Election had 65,000 Ohio voters switched, favoring the Democratic Party candidate.) If there is no such candidate, the Electoral College winner becomes the next US President. If neither candidate exists, the House of Representatives chooses a US President as the Twelfth Amendment directs. Should less than 50% of all eligible voters vote, signaling that a majority of voters either do not care or believe that the candidates do not deserve their votes, either the Electoral College or the House of Representatives elects a US President according to the existing election rules.

Only with more than 50% of all eligible voters voting, may these new election rules—building on the existing ones—benefit society in close elections. As mentioned earlier in this chapter, a) the requirement that more than fifty percent of all eligible voters must vote to make the nationwide popular vote a decisive factor in electing a US President and b) keeping the existing election system as a back-up differentiate these rules from the Federal System Plan of 1970.

Under the rules of the modified election system, all states become vital for both major party candidates. To win the nationwide popular vote, both candidates are likely to compete in large states. To win in at least 26 states, both candidates are likely to compete in small states. As close elections can hardly be won inside only 28 large and small states, both candidates are likely to compete in medium states as well. In contrast, due to the "winner-take-all" principle, most large and small states are "safe" for either candidate, and they are almost ignored in the "battleground-kind" election campaigns, except for fundraising purposes.

Under these new rules, nobody seems to lose. Small states retain what they enjoy under the Electoral College and gain by becoming vital for winning in at least 26 states. Large states gain as the "winner-take-all" principle will not waste votes favoring the state's runner-up, so both major candidates are likely to compete there. Medium states do not lose, as they remain valuable should the Electoral College decide the election outcome, and gain by being a source for both the popular vote and prospective 26 "victorious" states. As a result, election campaigns are likely to be run by both major parties in all the states.

Both the nationwide popular vote and the "one state, one vote" principle become decisive in electing a President. The latter addresses federalist concerns [2], [25] in determining whether there is a "President of the states" in the election according to the direct popular will of the states. In contrast, in the existing election system, the "one state, one vote" principle is applied only if a US President is elected by the US Congress. Moreover, in this case, the will of a state can be expressed only via the state delegation in the House of Representatives.

Though the chances of multi-candidate elections do not seem to increase due to retaining the Electoral College, various ranked-choice voting schemes and approval voting [33] can, eventually, be used in determining the election winner both nationwide and in the states should such elections occur.

As mentioned earlier in this chapter, introducing the modified election system implies amending the US Constitution. This amendment should address a) details of the new election rules, b) detected flaws in the US Constitution that may cause weird election outcomes (see Chapter 2) and even a constitutional crisis (see Chapter 3), and c) the automatic plan of counting electoral votes, eliminating the "faithless elector problem."

One can also expect that this amendment will address the right of the American people to vote in US Presidential elections. As is well known, the US Constitution does not give American voters the right to vote for President (and Vice President). Moreover, in 2000, the US Supreme Court reaffirmed that the US Constitution does not guarantee American voters the right to vote even for presidential electors, no matter how egregious this may seem to the American electorate. (See The US Supreme Court decision on *Bush v. Gore* [34], the essay "The Right to Vote and Election 2000" [35], and the book "The Right

to Vote: The Contested History of Democracy in the United States"
[36].)

It seems that if the amendment gave the American people the right
to vote for President, there would no longer be a need for the right to
vote for presidential electors in the states. Due to incorporating the
automatic plan of counting "pseudo-electoral" votes in the modified
election system, votes cast by eligible state voters for President (and Vice
President) would determine to which candidate state "pseudo-electoral"
votes are to be awarded should the Electoral College mechanism
decide the election outcome. At the same time, state legislatures should
retain the right to appoint electors in the states, as Article 2 of the US
Constitution directs, when the voter turnout is negligible so that the
awarding of "pseudo-electoral" votes cannot be considered legitimate
(see the description of the modified election system earlier in this
chapter).

The author, however, would like to make it clear that the right to
vote in America is an extremely complicated matter [35], [36], and
the above reasoning is no more than a logically possible approach to
introducing this right in US Presidential elections. At the same time,
the right to vote in US Presidential elections should undoubtedly be
the key issue in any substantive discussion about possible changes in
the existing election system (or of this system) associated with making
the nationwide popular vote a decisive factor in electing a US President.
Readers interested in an introduction to the issue of the right to vote in
US Presidential elections are referred to the essay "The Right to Vote
and Election 2000" [35].

The Founding Fathers devised the Electoral College as part of
a compromise keeping states of free settlers together as a nation. As
mentioned earlier, by leaving key issues of this election mechanism
unaddressed, they might have believed that new generations of

Americans would propose a better election system or at least a better compromise as the country developed, rather than debating the Electoral College for more than two centuries.

The proposed modified election system seems to be such a new and better ("win-win") compromise, always giving the Federation of states a chance to elect its Chief Executive by the nation as a whole and motivating more Americans to vote in US Presidential elections.

Conclusion

The system of electing a US President is unique and very logically designed. This system appeared as a compromise attained by the Constitutional Convention participants in 1787. However, some ideas underlying this compromise turned out to have been effective for more than two centuries. Numerous attempts to change the system have been made over more than 200 years. Making the nationwide popular will the top priority in determining outcomes of US Presidential elections was the purpose of many of these attempts. The attempts reflect a historic transformation of the loosely associated states of free settlers into a unified society. As a result of the transformation, the American electorate seems to consistently favor the election of a Chief Executive of the Union by a mandate from the entire nation. However, the implementation of such an inclination requires changing the US Constitution.

The existing system possesses features that may be viewed both as its merits and as its deficiencies by some US voters. For instance, under certain assumptions, the system guarantees that a US President can always be elected without run-off elections (see Chapter 1). This guarantee, however, requires the mechanism for electing a US President in the US Congress. While some US voters view the absence of the run-offs as a merit of the system, many US voters consider this mechanism as a disadvantage.

The existing system is complicated to understand in depth. This complexity might contribute to the fact that more than 40% of US voters do not usually vote in US Presidential elections. In addition, the system contains certain discrepancies that have remained unaddressed.

The author believes that US voters deserve clear explanations of how the system works, why it works as it does, what possible alternatives to this system are, and to what extent these alternatives are better or worse than the existing election system. Employing logical analysis both in public education and in the discussion of the elections in the media may help make these explanations. However, while solutions to many election problems derive from their logical analysis, some of these problems still can be discussed only at the level of subjectivity and personal preferences.

Applying logical analysis even to the latter group of problems could, nevertheless, make a difference. This is how discussion of the election system in the media could become more understandable to a broad spectrum of US residents. Also, interested people can view this discussion as an opportunity to improve their analytical skills in general and critically evaluate statements of recognized scholars in the field. Certainly, the penetration of logical analysis into society through this "channel" could convince more US voters to participate in future US Presidential elections.

Logical analysis can also help find answers to two questions on the election system presented in the Preface. In particular, the following simple observations may be helpful:

First, the election system that was initially designed by the Constitutional Convention participants and the current one are two different systems. Therefore, denying any alternatives to the current election system on the grounds of deviating from the ideas of the Founding Fathers does not seem justifiable.

Second, making changes in the election system, as well as replacing this system with another one, is not prohibited by the US Constitution.

Third, in 1816, Thomas Jefferson said: "Some men ascribe to the men of a preceding age a wisdom more than human, and suppose what they did to be beyond amendment. *** I am certainly not an advocate for frequent and untried changes in laws and constitutions. *** But I know also, that laws and institutions must go hand in hand with the progress of the human mind." [31]

Fourth, the existing system has evolved as a result of a compromise. By leaving certain key issues unaddressed in the US Constitution, the Founding Fathers might have expected that new generations of Americans would develop a better election system or at least would suggest a better compromise.

Fifth, a new election system may replace the old one only if this new system is at least no worse than the old system. Therefore, any reasonable advances in reforming the existing election system can be made only if criteria for comparing presidential election systems were available. These criteria should be developed by social scientists, explained to US voters by political leaders and the media, and accepted by society. Certainly, these criteria should take into consideration various factors. The existing perception of what US Presidential candidate should be elected to the office of US President is one such factor. One should not, however, expect in advance that a particular system would prevail as a result of the public discussion of the election systems in the years to come. Nevertheless, the discussion should examine all the proposed systems.

Sixth, the detected discrepancies in the existing system should be addressed and corrected, which would require certain changes in this system. In particular, it seems that persons whom US voters expect electors to vote in favor of and persons whom electors cast their votes in favor of should be the same, which is not guaranteed by the existing election rules.

Finally, certain requirements should be met in order to take the direct popular will into consideration in determining outcomes of US Presidential elections. From the author's viewpoint, one can speak about the expressed direct will of the people and about that of 50 states in a US Presidential election only if, respectively,

a) more than 50% of all eligible US voters voted in the election, and

b) more than 50% of all eligible US voters residing in each of at least 26 places (states and DC) voted in the election.

These requirements may strengthen the incentive to vote in US Presidential elections in the American electorate. Introducing these requirements implies conducting a nationwide census of all US voters rather than that of only the voting-age population. Holding US Presidential elections under these requirements could determine whether a US Presidential candidate can receive a mandate to govern from the nation in a US Presidential election.

If requirement a) is not met in the election, US voters may better understand why the Founding Fathers developed the election system to be independent of the nationwide will, and why the Electoral College mechanism can be viewed as a protective election mechanism [1].

How reasonable or how unreasonable are the existing rules of US Presidential elections? To answer this question, one should comprehend what options to win the elections these rules leave to US Presidential candidates. Among three such options, analyzed in Chapter 4, at least one may be viewed as a consequence of the "loopholes" in the existing election system. These "loopholes" exist due to certain fuzzy rules of US Presidential elections. However, some readers may object that what is not prohibited by the US Constitution and Federal Statutes should be allowed for US Presidential candidates. Thus, the American electorate should either accept nontraditional but not constitutionally prohibited options to win the US Presidency or change the election rules.

Unless electoral votes are won by more than two US Presidential candidates, some extreme situations considered in this book are mostly of theoretical interest. However, these situations may become a reality once non-major political parties and independent candidates recognize the importance of winning one or two electoral votes in the states of Maine and Nebraska, especially in close elections. It may happen if, for instance, non-major political parties nominate their US Presidential and US Vice Presidential candidates from these two states.

References

1. Belenky, A. Extreme Outcomes of US Presidential Elections: The Logic of appearance, Examples, Approaches to Eliminating, NISTRAMAN Consulting, Brookline, MA, 2003.

2. Hardaway, R. The Electoral College and the Constitution: The Case for Preserving Federalism, Praeger Publishers, Westport, CT, 1994.

3. Preserving Our Institutions. The Continuity of Congress. The First Report of the Continuity of the Government Commission. An American Enterprise Institute and Brookings Institution Project, American Enterprise Institute, 2003.

4. Farrand, M. (ed). The Records of the Federal Constitutional Convention of 1787 in 4 volumes, New Haven, 1911.

5. The Constitution of the United States of America – 1787, United States Code, vol. 1. United States Government Printing Office, Washington, 1989.

6. Berns, W. (ed) After the People Vote: a Guide to the Electoral College, The AEI Press, Washington DC, 1992.

7. Peirce, N., Longley, L. The Electoral College Primer 2000, Yale University Press, New Haven and London, 1999.

8. Peirce, N. The People's President. The Electoral College in American History and the Direct-Vote Alternative, Simon & Shuster, NY, 1968.

9. Schumaker P., Loomis B. (ed). Choosing a President. The Electoral College and Beyond, Chatham House Publishers, Seven Bridges Press, LLC, New York, London, 2002.

10. Peirce, N., Longley, L. The People's President. The Electoral College in American History and the Direct-Vote Alternative. Revised edition. Yale University Press, 1981.

11. Feerick, J. The Electoral College: why it was created. American Bar Association Journal, March 1968, vol.54, 249–255.

12. Belenky, A. An elementary analysis of some mathematical concepts employed in and relations associated with Amendment 12 of the US Constitution. Mathematical and Computer Modelling, vol.39, 123-132, 2004.

13. Kimberling, W. The Electoral College. National Clearinghouse in Election Administration. Federal Election Committee, 1992.

14. Maine Revised Statues Annotated, Title 21-A, Chapter 9, Subchapter 5, West, 1974.

15. Nebraska Revised State Statues, 32-1038, 32-714 Reviser of Statues, State of Nebraska, 2000.

16. 343 U.S. 214. United States Government Printing Office, Washington, 1953.

17. 146 U.S. 1. United States Government Printing Office, Washington, 1953.

18. Congressional Quarterly's Guide to U.S. Elections. Second Edition. Congressional Quarterly, Inc., 1984.

19. Statistical Abstract of the United States. The National Data Book, Bureau of Census, 2002.

20. Belenky, A. Winning the US Presidency: Rules of the Game and Playing by the Rules. NISTRAMAN Consulting, Brookline, MA, 2004.

21. Federal Register. US Electoral College. www.archives. gov/federal register/electoral college/electoral college/html Internet, December, 2002.

22. The Charter & Bylaws of the Democratic Party of the United States as Amended by the Democratic National Committee, January 19, 2002 www.democrats.org/pdfs/ charter.pdf/ Internet, December, 2002.

23. The Rules of the Republican Party as Adopted by the 2000 Republican National Convention, July 13, 2000 www.rnc.org/gopinfo/ rules, Internet, December, 2002.

24. Congressional Record-Senate 1968—1970.

25. Best, J. The Choice of the People? Debating the Electoral College. Rowman & Littlefiled Publishers, Inc., Lanham, MD, 1996.

26. Banzhaf, J. III. One man, 3.312 votes: a mathematical analysis of the Electoral College. Villanova Law Review, vol. 13, 304–332, 1968.

27. American Enterprise Institute for Public Policy Research. Proposals for Revision of the Electoral College System, Washington D.C., 1969.

28. Rife, D. Pledge of Allegiance. Teaching & Learning Company, Carthage, IL, 1998.

29. Bennett, R. Popular election of the President without a Constitutional Amendment. In the book: Jacobson, A. and Rosenfeld, M. (ed.) The Longest Night. Politics and Perspectives on Election

2000, 391-396, University of California Press, Berkeley, Los Angeles, London, 2002.

30. A. Schlessinger, Jr., Fixing the Electoral College. The Washington Post, December 19, 2000, p.A39.

31. Congressional Record-Senate, Tuesday, January 20, 1966. United States Government Printing Office, Washington, 1966.

32. Congressional Record-Senate, Friday, February 21, 1966. United States Government Printing Office, Washington, 1966.

33. Brams, S., Fishburn, P. Approval Voting. Birkhauser, Boston/Basel/Stuttgart, 1983.

34. 121 U.S. 526, 529. United States Government Printing Office, Washington 2000.

35. Keyssar, A. The Right to vote and Election 2000. In Rakove, J. (ed.) The Unfinished Election of 2000, Basic Books, New York, 2001.

36. Keyssar, A. The Right to Vote: The Contested History of Democracy in the United States, Basic Books, New York, 2000.

About the author

Alexander S. Belenky is Visiting scholar at the MIT Center for Engineering Systems Fundamentals. He is the author of books and scientific articles in the field of optimization and game theory and their applications. His recent books include *Extreme Outcomes of US Presidential Elections* (2003) and *Winning the US Presidency: Rules of the Game and Playing by the Rules* (2004). His recent articles include *The 2004 Election: Local Polls and Campaign Strategies* (2004), *The 2004 Election: How It Can Be Won* (2004), *Competitive Strategies of U.S. Presidential Candidates in Election Campaigns* (2005), *Calculating the Minimal Fraction of the Popular Vote To Win the U.S. Presidency in the Electoral College* (2005), *To Queue or Not To Queue? In a U.S. presidential election, that should NOT be a question!* (with Richard C. Larson) (2006*), Voting shouldn't require a heroic act of patience* (with Richard C. Larson) (2006), *Faulty system for democracy* (with Richard C. Larson) (2007). He was an invited guest on radio and TV talk shows throughout the country in the course of the 2004 Election campaign.

Alexander S. Belenky holds two M. S. degrees (in engineering and in mathematics), Ph.D. in systems analysis and mathematics, and D.Sc. in applications of mathematical methods. He also holds the academic rank of Professor of applications of mathematical methods.

Printed in the United States
112198LV00007B/347/A

9 781420 848540